ALL ABOUT
MY NEIGHBOURHOOD

Written by Andrew Burrell

NURSERY WORLD

TES
THE TIMES EDUCATIONAL SUPPLEMENT

NURSERY WORLD

TES
THE TIMES EDUCATIONAL SUPPLEMENT

Managing Editor Patricia Grogan
Art Editor Sally Smallwood

DTP Design Alternative View Studios
Photography Andy Crawford

Editor Louise Pritchard
Editorial assistant Edward FitzGerald

Consultant Marian Whitehead

First published in Great Britain in 1999 by
Times Supplements Limited
Admiral House, 66–68 East Smithfield, London E1 9XY

Copyright © 1999 Times Supplements Limited, London

All rights reserved. No part of this publication may be reproduced, stored in a retrieval system or transmitted in any form or by any means, electronic, mechanical, photocopying, recording or otherwise, without the prior written permission of the copyright owner.

A CIP catalogue record for this book is available from the British Library

ISBN 1-84122-002-7

Colour reproduction by Prima Creative Services, UK
Printed and bound in Belgium by Proost

Nursery World would like to thank the children and staff at the following Nurseryworks nurseries for taking part in this book:
Broadgate Nursery, London EC2
Billets Corner Nursery, London E17

CONTENTS

4–13
*Introduction and
How to use this book*

14–19
Chapter 1
My home

20–25
Chapter 2
Other homes

26–31
Chapter 3
Around my home

32–39
Chapter 4
Visiting the park

40–45
Chapter 5
At the shops

46–53
Chapter 6
Journeys

54–61
Chapter 7
Out and about

62–63
Resources & template

64
*Index and
acknowledgments*

INTRODUCTION

All About My Neighbourhood contains more than 100 activities divided into seven chapters. Each chapter explores one avenue of the book's central theme. The activities are self contained but also build on from each other, so you can either dip into several chapters when planning your theme or you can use complete chapters. The activities are firmly underpinned by seven areas of learning to help you incorporate them into your planning. The topic web on pages 12–13 shows you into which areas of learning each activity falls and each activity has symbols representing the areas of learning covered.

Planning a curriculum

The activities in this book have been devised using principles of good practice identified in early-years guidelines throughout the United Kingdom. It is a widely held belief that children of nursery age learn most effectively through play.

There are many reasons for using play in early-years settings. Firstly, children's ideas and interests are often central to their play. This gives children a sense of ownership in their learning. Play can also be very motivating and thus enhance children's learning. Its practical nature allows children to explore and experiment at first hand. A primary function of play is that it helps children to develop their social and language skills. Play is also often considered a natural activity that is appropriate in the development of young children. Play can assist in meeting children's individual needs and it provides a context in which children can reflect and act out difficult experiences in a safe environment.

Opportunities for child-led play should exist and be identified in curriculum planning. Many of the activities in this book give extension ideas for this kind of learning. It is important, however, to realise that the activities suggested in this book do not represent a complete curriculum. Young children need to follow a broad and balanced curriculum that is also relevant to their personal needs. The purpose of this book is to assist in the development of such a curriculum.

Two important things to consider when planning are differentiation and equal opportunities. Much of the quality of your teaching and children's learning depends upon your ability to be aware of the responses of individuals and to consider them in your planning. Take into account possible differences between children to give them all the best opportunity to learn. You also need to ensure that each child has equal access and opportunity to all aspects of the nursery. Monitor this carefully, encouraging children to use equipment they would not normally be drawn to.

Each activity in this book covers one or more of the following areas of learning: Personal and Social Development, Language and Literacy, Mathematics, Science and Technology, Time and Place, Creative Development, Physical Development.

Personal and Social Development

The suggested activities reflect the belief that the nursery has a critical role to play in the personal and social development of young children. This includes the development of personal values and an understanding of self and others. Development in this area is important if children are to be confident, show self-respect and have the ability to establish effective relationships with other children and also with adults.

Children need to learn, for example, how to share, take turns, show interest in and play with other children. They need to learn how to make friends, accept guidance and direction from adults and to concentrate on and complete tasks. Skills in this area of learning need to meet personal needs such as dressing oneself and handling a knife and fork.

To develop fully, children must practise personal and social skills in a variety of nursery situations. Working in groups of varying sizes, for instance, teaches children to be co-operative.

Language and Literacy

Children of nursery age need to learn to communicate effectively through speech and gesture. Speaking and listening should be central to the care and education of young children. This book emphasises the role of speech in the learning process. Speech should be reciprocal and often initiated and led by the child. The activities engage children in a variety of stimulating learning opportunities through which they can communicate their thoughts and feelings to others. They provide plenty of scope for children to listen and respond to stories, songs, nursery rhymes and poems. Opportunities also exist for children to make up their own stories and to take part in role play.

Nursery staff should ensure they build on the rich language experiences and skills that children possess on their entry to the nursery. By listening and talking in groups children can explore and share their experiences and those of others.

It is important that you give careful consideration to all four modes of language. These should be viewed as complementary to one another. Recent research has identified the importance of children's sensitivity to rhyme as they develop listening and reading skills. Nursery rhymes and stories with rhyming text are often suggested in this book as starting points for activities.

The activities in this book also give careful consideration to the various purposes for which writing is used. Children are encouraged to participate in various mark-making activities. Adults can support children's emergent writing through sensitive intervention and encouragement.

Mathematics

This book endeavours to present mathematics as an enjoyable experience. Children should encounter mathematics through a range of activities. Guided play with materials such as sand and water provide children with important information about volume and capacity. Role-play situations, such as setting up a shop, can also give rise to mathematical experiences. They provide opportunities to share personal experiences and to develop mathematical language in a more meaningful context. Visits around the children's neighbourhood provide valuable opportunities for the children to develop their mathematical understanding; children can be encouraged to identify and recognise different shapes in their environment.

Mathematical language can also be explored through singing number rhymes, which can provide useful starting points for other areas of learning. Many of the activities in this book are intended to help children learn about common prepositions, such as in, out, on top, underneath, in front, behind and next to. Ensure you introduce and reinforce mathematical language in all appropriate situations.

Science and Technology

When exploring science and technology, ensure you capitalise on young children's curiosity and interest in the world around them. Activities centred on play and talk can also be used to develop a range of scientific skills. Many of the activities in this book encourage children to develop their observation skills. They encourage children to look for patterns and to classify objects according to various criteria. Children's observations can help them make predictions, and adults in the nursery can support this through the use of appropriate questions. Some of the activities aim to develop children's problem-solving skills by, for example, considering how they might make their own bridge constructions stronger. Others promote the development and understanding of a variety of scientific concepts such as rough and smooth. You can use some activities to help children develop an understanding of health-related issues including food and hygiene. These should be developed in meaningful contexts. Children can also be encouraged to extend their understanding of the weather and other aspects of the natural world through first-hand experiences. There are opportunities for children to explore different materials as they create their own models. Through these kinds of activity children can begin to consider and select the materials that they think are most appropriate for a particular task. Appropriate questioning can help children evaluate their work and challenge their thinking. All the activities aim to develop a positive attitude towards enquiry.

Time and Place

This area of learning is concerned with people – how they live, their relationships with each other and the environment, both in the past and in the present. The activities help children to understand these concepts by relating them to themselves, their families and their environment. Young children's learning should be embedded in what is familiar to them; curriculum provision should reflect the cultural diversity of the neighbourhood in which the children live. The activities have been written with the belief that young children learn effectively through first-hand experiences. Suggestions are given for visits to various places in the local environment to support this.

Both in the nursery and when on outings, children can learn about the work of a range of people, including postal workers, shopkeepers, fire-fighters, nurses and other people employed locally who the children see at work in their everyday lives. Finally, remember that stories also provide a powerful medium for developing children's understanding of time and place.

Creative Development

This topic is concerned with developing children's imagination and improving their ability to communicate and express ideas and feelings in a range of creative ways. Children should have regular opportunities for both two- and three-dimensional work; this belief is reflected in the range and type of activity suggested in this book. The activities encourage children to use a wide variety of materials, tools, instruments and other resources in their play. Young children should also have opportunities for imaginative role play. Role-play activities will encourage children to use their imagination through art, music, stories and play. Such experiences can contribute to growth in self-confidence and the ability to identify with others and discover new ways of understanding.

Physical Development

This area of learning is concerned with developing children's physical control; manipulative skills indoors and outdoors; mobility and awareness of space. Space must be available on a regular and extended basis throughout the day.

Careful thought needs to be given to the equipment used for physical play. It should include simple but versatile materials such as sand, planks and crates. Children also need access to covers, blankets, tents and other props to stimulate imaginative and physical play. Fine motor skills can be developed by handling tools, instruments and malleable materials. Many activities in this book encourage the development of construction skills through building, assembling, lifting, carrying and arranging objects. Other skills addressed include those concerned with mobility and agility.

The book aims to broaden and extend children's physical experiences in a variety of contexts through a range of activities. Ideas are given for providing situations for sharing resources, collaborating, making judgements, solving problems and using language.

Assessing Children's Learning

Assessment, planning and teaching need to form a continuous cycle in which one part informs the next. Careful observation and assessment can provide useful insights into children's understanding and their achievements. This information can then be used to provide appropriate activities for future learning.

When planning acitvities, it is important to consider the learning that you *intend* to take place. This, in itself, should be informed through regular assessement. In other words, assessment is a tool that forms an integral part of the teaching and learning process. It is also important to remember that children do not always learn exactly what we expect. We need to be sensitive to what the children have actually learnt. This can include the unintended as well as the unexpected.

You may find it helpful to identify assessment opportunities and to include these in weekly planning. Draw up a checklist of expected outcomes leaving space for comments. The expected outcomes should be kept to a minimum, so effective and focused observation can take place. Select no more than two learning outcomes at a time to help keep the assessment manageable.

Observations need to include insights into what the

children actually do. They also need to focus on how the children interact with each other; this is particularly important in relation to personal and social development outcomes. It is sometimes useful to record what the children say and also how they may feel about a particular activity. Children's learning is demonstrated in a variety of ways including how they work with materials, and what they draw, write and make.

Questioning forms an important part of assessing children. Asking open-ended questions can provide valuable information about children's understanding. These questions should do the following:
- lead the children to review ideas – 'Why did that happen?'
- promote investigation – 'Which of these materials are waterproof?'
- ask the children to justify their ideas – 'Why do you think that?'
- encourage self-evaluation – 'How strong do you think your bridge is?' 'Can you think of any ways in which you could improve it?'
- provide information about children's understanding and misunderstanding – 'How does it work?'

Carrying out assessment has important implications for classroom management. Children not involved in the assessment must be able to play or work independently or work with another adult whilst the assessment is being carried out. Insights into the children's learning should be recorded either during or immediately after each observation. Finally, ensure you establish links between activities so that children's learning becomes deeper and more meaningful than would be the case if they were presented with a series of isolated activities.

Visiting the local neighbourhood

It is extremely important that young children have an opportunity to visit their neighbourhood when they are engaged in many of the activities in this book. Young children begin exploring the world they live in long before they enter the nursery and other pre-school settings. Their recognition of distinctive places, surroundings and people is evident in their play, conversation and drawings.

Learning through a theme
A theme centred on the children's own neighbourhood therefore provides a valuable opportunity to reinforce and extend this previous learning. Additionally, it enables all children to make a personal contribution based on their own experiences. Everyday activities in which children participate can be discussed. Visits to relatives, the shops and the doctor, for example, involve the children in different journeys around their neighbourhood.

The nursery setting itself is part of the local environment. It is through familiarity with the nursery that children begin to find their way around. They also become accustomed to the different patterns of daily movement and activity.

Learning in the nursery must be underpinned by first-hand encounters with other places and features in the children's neighbourhood. This provides young children with opportunities to observe and explore the relationships other people have with their surroundings. Most activities in this book have been devised with this in mind. They seek to demonstrate the wealth of curriculum potential in undertaking visits in the neighbourhood. What can be done in any particular nursery will of course be influenced by the kinds of opportunity that exist in the immediate environment. All nurseries have many places of potential interest that are easily accessible. Interesting places to explore might include a road, park, shopping centre, wood or railway station.

Exploring the local neighbourhood provides children with an opportunity to talk about where they and their families live. It can help them to extend their awareness of the local surroundings. Children can be helped to identify specific features of the environment such as buildings, and to explore selected areas such as the park or shops.

Exploring familiar surroundings should link closely with the children's own experiences, capabilities and interests. Learning at first-hand can bring a new sense of awareness to familiar surroundings. It also provides opportunities for individual forms of self-expression. A variety of different skills can be reinforced through visits to the local environment. Social skills, for example, are involved as children share equipment and resources.

Children must learn to follow and respond to instructions given out by nursery staff and adult helpers when out in the neighbourhood. Visits around the local environment bring the children into close contact with other people. They can help children to understand the different contributions people make to their local environment.

Preparing for visits

All visits must be carefully planned. It is important to decide how the visit fits into the overall development of the theme. Some visits will be most appropriate at the start of a suggested activity. In this way they provide a useful stimulus for further work. In other instances it may be appropriate for a visit to be undertaken after some initial work has been carried out with the children in the nursery.

Nursery staff must always visit the location in advance before taking the children there on a trip. This will enable you to consider the potential learning opportunities and to consider safety aspects, such as crossing roads. A preliminary visit to the park, for example, would allow you to observe play apparatus, wildlife, interesting trees and plants, and find space for games and a picnic. It will also give you the opportunity to find out where amenities such as toilets are located.

Consult the nursery's policy on taking children beyond the nursery building. A letter home to the children's parents or carers needs to give details of the visit. Include information on appropriate clothes and footwear to be worn and any food or drink to be taken. Arrange for extra help so that the children can be divided into very small groups.

On the day of the visit take with you and leave in the nursery a list of the names of children and adults who are going on the visit. Talk to the adults about the purpose of the visit and your expectations before setting off. Provide each helper with a list of the children they need to supervise. It is often useful not to have a group yourself so that you can move easily from one group to another. Each child could wear a name badge. Take the telephone number of the nursery and a first aid pack in case of minor accidents.

tracing houses

tracing

Before going outside, talk to the children about the purpose of the visit and what you are hoping they will see and find out about. Provide an opportunity for the children to ask any questions. Talk to them about your safety rules and the reasons why they are needed. Finally, before setting off ensure all children are given the opportunity to go to the toilet and remember to always count the children and adults before you leave any area to ensure no one is left behind.

Visitors to the nursery

Finally, do not overlook the possibility of asking a visitor into the nursery. This can provide useful links with the wider community. In some instances it may be possible to arrange for an appropriate person to come and talk to the children, when a visit cannot be made. Visitors may include those employed in familiar occupations such as fire-fighters, postal workers, bakers, nurses or police officers. It is of course important not to reinforce gender stereotyping when talking about people's occupations.

Asking questions

Consider carefully the types of question you ask. Questions can be broadly divided into two main types: open and closed. Throughout this book, questions are suggested. The majority of these are the open type. Open questions differ from closed questions by inviting a range of acceptable, often longer, responses. Closed questions in contrast only require short responses. A typical closed question would be, 'Do you like visiting the park?' This question invites only a very short response, probably either 'yes' or 'no'.

Closed questions have many disadvantages over the open variety. The majority of closed questions have only one correct or anticipated answer. They can engender the idea in children that learning is about finding 'the one correct answer'. They can also, through repeated use, lead to children to guess the answer or word that they think the adult is expecting.

In contrast, open questions require more planning. Children also need longer to formulate their responses. Open questions require more complex management in large group situations as they invite more diverse and longer responses than closed questions.

Open questions can offer more opportunities for creative thinking. They may provide more insight into individual children's understanding. They can also be used to guide children to another step in their learning. Open questions can challenge children's thinking and motivate them to become actively involved in activities. Open questions can also be effective in developing certain skills. During storytime, for example, the adult may ask a child to predict by asking what they think will happen next.

How to use this book

All About My Neighbourhood is divided into seven self-contained chapters that develop one avenue of the book's central theme. Each chapter has its own coloured band, to help you identify which chapter you are in, and its own contents list. The contents list gives you a summary of each activity to help you decide which activities to use. The materials needed for each activity are always found at the top left of the activity and the educational aims are nearby.

Educational symbols

Each activity introduces one or more areas of learning. The symbols show you which areas are covered and the accompanying text gives you the specific aims.

 This symbol shows the activity will develop aspects of language and literacy

 This symbol shows the activity will develop aspects of science and technology

 This symbol shows the activity will develop aspects of creative development

 This symbol shows the activity will develop aspects of mathematics

 This symbol shows the activity will develop aspects of personal and social development

 This symbol shows the activity will develop aspects of physical development

 This symbol shows the activity will develop aspects of time and place

Each activity is numbered for easy reference.

The triangle and circle show you the suggested adult–child ratio for the activity.

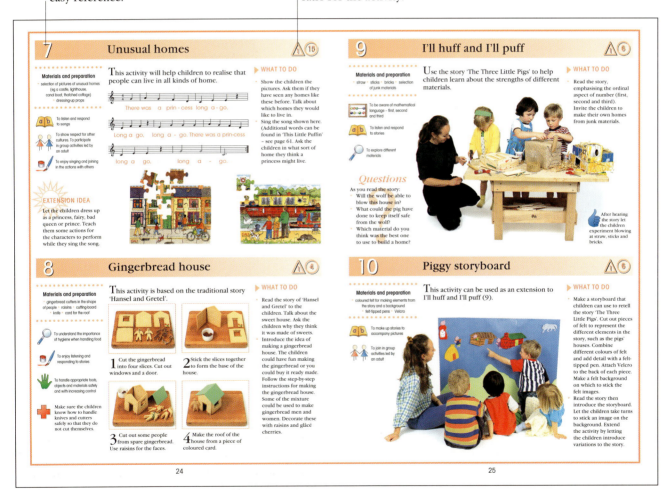

Additional symbols

Many activities have additional hints and tips or safety points. They are identified by the symbols shown below.

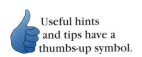 Useful hints and tips have a thumbs-up symbol.

 Safety points have a red cross symbol.

Breaking down the information

Each activity either has step-by-step instructions or bullet-pointed instructions under the heading 'What To Do'. Many activities have suggested questions and extension ideas, also under the appropriate headings.

 TIP One or more helpful suggestions for increasing an activity's learning value have a star symbol.

Topic web

Each activity in this book is underpinned by one or more of the areas of learning. This topic web lists all the activities that contribute to the different areas of learning. The web can therefore be used as a tool for planning and providing a balanced curriculum that is both challenging and enjoyable for children in a wide range of early-years settings.

 ## CREATIVE DEVELOPMENT

- Through my window (3) page 16
- Simple house cards (7) page 18
- A garden in miniature (9) page 19
- Make a den (3) page 22
- Make a house (4) page 22
- Brick patterns (5) page 23
- Unusual homes (7) page 24
- Gingerbread house (8) page 24
- At the doctor's (9) page 31
- Make fire-fighters' hats (8) page 30
- Who lives in the park? (6) page 35
- Sounds (9) page 37
- Looking at leaf textures (12) page 39
- Leaf printing (13) page 39
- Eating out (2) page 41
- Being a baker (4) page 42
- All aboard (4) page 48
- Little Red Riding Hood (7) page 50
- Make a story map (11) page 52
- Travel agents (13) page 53
- Weather (7) page 58
- I can see a rainbow (14) page 61

 ## PERSONAL AND SOCIAL DEVELOPMENT

- Through my window (3) page 16
- My family (6) page 17
- Other homes (1) page 21
- Make a den (3) page 22
- Building houses (6) page 23
- Unusual homes (7) page 24
- Piggy storyboard (10) page 25
- Bridge shapes (4) page 28
- Visiting a postbox (10) page 30
- These people help us (7) page 30
- Make fire-fighters' hats (8) page 30
- At the doctor's (9) page 31
- Visiting a post box (10) page 31
- The park (1) page 33
- Bird feeder (7) page 36
- Wild animal picnic (11) page 38
- I went to the shops and bought (1) page 41
- Eating out (2) page 41
- Which shop? (5) page 43
- People carriers (2) page 47
- Trains, boats and aeroplanes (3) page 48
- All aboard (4) page 48
- The wheels on the bus (5) page 49
- Little Red Riding Hood (7) page 50
- Traffic lights game (8) page 50
- Finding your way (10) page 51
- Blind man's buff (2) page 55
- Our friends (3) page 56
- Helping each other (4) page 56
- Posting letters (6) page 57
- Keeping cool (11) page 60

 ## MATHEMATICS

- My front door (2) page 15
- Through my window (3) page 16
- Inside homes (2) page 21
- Make a house (4) page 22
- Brick patterns (5) page 23
- I'll huff and I'll puff (9) page 25
- My neighbourhood (1) page 27
- Where do they live? (5) page 35
- Flying high (8) page 36
- Wild animal picnic (11) page 38
- The baker's shop (3) page 42
- Being a baker (4) page 42
- Packaging (6) page 43
- Round or long? (7) page 44
- Heavy or light? (8) page 44
- People carriers (2) page 47
- Here comes the bus (6) page 49
- Finding your way (10) page 51
- Which comes first? (1) page 55
- Posting letters (6) page 57
- Keeping dry (9) page 59
- Is it waterproof? (10) page 59
- Keeping cool (11) page 60
- Which clothes? (12) page 60

Science and technology

- My home (1) page 15
- Rough or smooth? (4) page 16
- Simple house cards (7) page 18
- How does your garden grow? (8) page 18
- Make a den (3) page 22
- Building houses (6) page 23
- Gingerbread house (8) page 24
- I'll huff and I'll puff (9) page 25
- Tall towers (2) page 27
- Building bridges (3) page 28
- Fun at the park (2) page 33
- Slides in the park (3) page 34
- What makes the best slide? (4) page 34
- Who lives in the park? (6) page 35
- Bird feeder (7) page 36
- Flying high (8) page 36
- Sounds (9) page 37
- Wild animal picnic (11) page 38
- Being a baker (4) page 42
- Packaging (6) page 43
- Round or long? (7) page 44
- Make a story map (11) page 52
- Special clothes (5) page 57
- Weather (7) page 58
- Rainy days (8) page 58
- Is it waterproof? (10) page 59
- Keeping cool (11) page 60
- Which clothes? (12) page 60
- Finding out about the wind (13) page 61
- I can see a rainbow (14) page 61

Physical development

- This is my little house (5) page 17
- Inside homes (2) page 21
- Brick patterns (5) page 23
- Gingerbread house (8) page 24
- Tall towers (2) page 27
- Building bridges (3) page 28
- Bridge shapes (4) page 28
- Photograph puzzles (5) page 29
- Make fire fighters' hats (8) page 30
- Fun at the park (2) page 33
- Slides in the park (3) page 34
- What makes the best slide? (4) page 34
- Who lives in the park? (6) page 35
- Flying high (8) page 36
- Leaf printing (13) page 39
- Packaging (6) page 43
- Trains, boats and aeroplanes (3) page 48
- Traffic lights patterns (9) page 51
- Finding your way (10) page 51
- Blind man's buff (2) page 55
- Our friends (3) page 56
- Keeping dry (9) page 59
- Keeping cool (11) page 60
- Which clothes? (12) page 60

Language and literacy

- My home (1) page 15
- Through my window (3) page 16
- This is my little house (5) page 17
- My family (6) page 17
- How does your garden grow? (8) page 18
- A garden in miniature (9) page 19
- Make a den (3) page 22
- Make a house (4) page 22
- Building houses (6) page 23
- Unusual homes (7) page 24
- I'll huff and I'll puff (9) page 25
- Piggy storyboard (10) page 25
- My neighbourhood (1) page 27
- Building bridges (3) page 28
- What's missing? (6) page 29
- These people help us (7) page 30
- At the doctor's (9) page 31
- Visiting a post box (10) page 31
- The park (1) page 33
- Sounds (9) page 37
- Similar sounds (10) page 37
- Wild animal picnic (11) page 38
- Looking at leaf textures (12) page 39
- I went to the shops and bought (1) page 41
- Eating out (2) page 41
- The baker's shop (3) page 42
- Which shop? (5) page 43
- Shopping lists (9) page 45
- Shopping bags (10) page 45
- Traffic watching (1) page 47
- People carriers (2) page 47
- All aboard (4) page 48
- The wheels on the bus (5) page 49
- Here comes the bus (6) page 49
- Little Red Riding Hood (7) page 50
- Traffic lights game (8) page 50
- Words everywhere (12) page 52
- Travel agents (13) page 53
- Which comes first? (1) page 55
- Helping each other (4) page 56
- Special clothes (5) page 57
- Weather (7) page 58
- Rainy days (8) page 58

Time and place

- My home (1) page 15
- Rough or smooth? (4) page 16
- This is my little house (5) page 17
- Other homes (1) page 21
- Inside homes (2) page 21
- My neighbourhood (1) page 27
- Building bridges (3) page 28
- Photograph puzzles (5) page 29
- What's missing? (6) page 29
- These people help us (7) page 30
- Visiting a postbox (10) page 31
- The park (1) page 33
- Fun at the park (2) page 33
- Where do they live? (5) page 35
- The baker's shop (3) page 42
- Which shop? (5) page 43
- Shopping lists (9) page 45
- Shopping bags (10) page 45
- Traffic watching (1) page 47
- Make a story map (11) page 52
- Words everywhere (12) page 52
- Travel agents (13) page 53
- Special clothes (5) 57
- Weather (7) page 58
- Rainy days (8) page 58
- Keeping Dry (9) 59
- Keeping cool (11) page 60
- Finding out about the wind (13) page 61
- I can see a rainbow (14) page 61

ALL ABOUT MY HOME

The activities in this chapter encourage children to think about their own homes and are intended to build on the children's existing understanding. Using children's homes as a starting point in activities, ensures all children can make valuable contributions to the activities. Finally, make yourself aware of the children's home environments and adapt activities as appropriate.

Activities in this chapter

1
My home
Children make books representing their homes using pictures cut out of catalogues. Each page represents a different room

2
My front door
Children are asked to think about differences and similarities by comparing their own front doors and other doors in the neighbourhood

3
Through my window
In this activity children are encouraged to record their observations by drawing pictures, which are then compiled into a class or group book

4
Rough or smooth?
Using a 'feely box', children are encouraged to think about rough and smooth surfaces and which they like best

5
This is my little house
Children learn the words and actions to a rhyme

6
My family
A discussion activity that encourages children to think about their families

7
Simple house cards
An activity in which children make cards to take home

8
How does your garden grow?
An activity that uses the popular nursery rhyme 'Mary, Mary, quite contrary' as a starting point for thinking about the needs of plants

9
A garden in miniature
A creative activity in which children think about gardens and make their own miniature gardens

1 My home

This book-making activity gives children the opportunity to talk about their homes.

Materials and preparation
- home-made books possibly in the shape of different homes a familiar book
- catalogues of household objects
- scissors • glue • writing equipment

 To learn about different types of home

 To learn how to use scissors appropriately

 To gain an understanding of common prepositions

Questions
- Do you have a favourite room or place in your home?
- Why is it your favourite room?
- In which room do you play/eat/sleep?

▶ WHAT TO DO
- Talk to the children about their homes.
- Show them a familiar book. Discuss what it contains – pages, pictures and words.
- Show the children the home-made books and the catalogues. Explain that they are going to make books about their homes.
- Ask them to cut out objects from the catalogues and stick them into their book. Each page could represent a different room.

👍 Find out what sort of home each child lives in before you begin and ensure you include appropriate reference material.

2 My front door

This activity encourages children to think about similarities and differences.

Materials and preparation
- paper • paints • felt-tipped pens • crayons

 To recognize when things are the same or different

EXTENSION IDEA
- Read 'Alfie Gets in First' by Shirley Hughes. Talk about what happens in the story. Show the children the lock on the nursery door and the key used to open it.
- Talk about the people who make regular visits to our front doors.

▶ WHAT TO DO
- Take the children for a walk around the neighbourhood. Encourage them to look carefully at doors. Point out the differences between the doors, for example some are old and some are new, some are painted and some are varnished wood. Draw the children's attention to a letter box or to a number on a door.
- Ask the children to describe their own front doors and scribe their descriptions.

👍 Make a display based around the children's own descriptions of their front door.

3 Through my window

Materials and preparation
- large home-made book in shh to stick the children's drawings
- drawing paper • crayons • coloured paper • pen • glue

 To show an increasing ability to observe

 To listen attentively and talk about experiences

 To participate in group activities led by an adult

 To recognise and name a range of shapes

👍 Show the children how to stick their picture into the book without using too much glue.

Start this activity by looking out of the nursery window and asking the children what they can see.

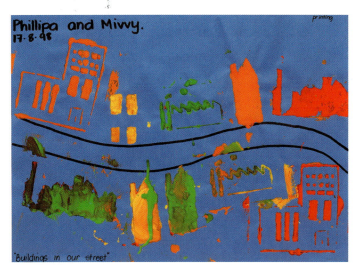

1. Ask the children to draw pictures of what they can see from their windows at home.

2. Stick each child's picture into the home-made book. Draw window frames around the pictures.

▶ WHAT TO DO
- Every page of the book could begin 'Through my window I can see …' Ask each child about his or her picture and write a sentence underneath the picture while the child watches to reinforce the left to right convention. Read back the sentence. Ask further questions, for example, 'What kinds of building can you see from a window at home?'

4 Rough or smooth?

Materials and preparation
- shoe box • variety of objects with a rough or smooth texture – small enough to fit inside the shoe box

 To talk about the immediate environment

 To learn the concepts of rough and smooth

Questions
- Which surface feels the roughest?
- Which surface feels the smoothest?
- Which surface do you like feeling best?
- What other things can you think of that are rough or smooth?

This activity encourages children to think about rough and smooth surfaces.

▶ WHAT TO DO
- Cut out a hole in the side of the shoe box large enough for the children to put their hands through to feel the objects. Choose some objects to put in the box.
- Consider surfaces in the nursery. Ask the children to feel the nursery floor. What does it feel like?
- Explore surfaces in the home corner. Ask the children to compare and contrast the various surfaces; which feel rough/smooth; which do you like/dislike?
- Show the children the 'feely box'. Ask them to close their eyes as you put each item in the box. Let them take it in turns to feel the objects and describe the textures.

5 This is my little house

  To recognise features in the world made by people

  To listen when others are speaking. To listen and respond to rhymes

  To perform actions to go with a rhyme

This rhyme provides a useful starting point for talking about the parts of a house.

My Little House Won't Stand Up Straight

My little house won't stand up straight,

My little house has lost its gate,

My little house bends up and down,

My little house is the oldest in town.

Here comes the wind; it blows and blows again.

Down falls my house. Oh, what a shame!

▶ **WHAT TO DO**

- Teach the children the rhyme and actions.
- Talk about the different parts of a house.

1 Touch fingertips to make a roof and rock the hands from side to side.

2 Drop two little fingers.

3 Rock the hands hard from side to side.

4 Blow through the thumbs. Drop the hands into the lap on the last line.

---

6 My family

Materials and preparation
- family photographs brought in by the children • home-made book • glue

  To show an interest in the experiences of others

  To talk freely with other children and familiar adults about their own experiences

TIP It is important that all children feel that their family unit is accepted and valued. Give the children a letter to take home requesting a photograph, or put up a notice inviting parents or carers to send one in.

Ask each child to bring in a photograph of their family.

1 Ask the children to stick their family photograph into the home-made book.

2 Write the children's comments next to the photograph of their families.

▶ **WHAT TO DO**

- Let the children have plenty of opportunity to talk about their family.
- Ask the children to think about the things they do with their family and then follow steps one and two.

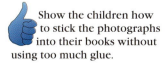

Show the children how to stick the photographs into their books without using too much glue.

7 Simple house cards

Materials and preparation
- A4 paper • envelopes • colouring pencils • crayons • scissors

 To explore colour and shape

 To use tools safely and with increasing control

EXTENSION IDEA
- Make house-shaped cards in which the children can write. To make a card, fold the paper in half. Fold two diagonals from the outside edge towards the folded edge to form a roof shape for the house. Children can then draw the outside features of their homes.
- Alternatively, cut the doors and windows in the children's pictures so that they can be opened and closed.

In this activity, children make a card to take home to give to someone in their family.

1 Lay all the materials on the table and ask the children to draw a picture of their home or a home they have seen near the nursery.

2 Ask the children to decorate the inside of their card by drawing their family. Some children may like to write inside, too.

▸ WHAT TO DO
- Before making the cards, take the children outside to look at some different homes nearby. What features can the children see? Roof, windows, doors and so on.
- Introduce the children to the idea of making a card for their family then follow steps one to three.

3 Give each child an envelope for their card. Ask them to address the envelope. Make stamps to stick on the front of each one. Let the children take home their cards.

8 How does your garden grow?

 To listen and respond to rhymes. To write their own names

 To understand that plants need certain things to stay alive

Questions
- What do plants need to be able to grow?
- What do you need to help you grow?
- Do you think your sunflower will be as tall as you?

This rhyme provides a starting point for talking about what plants need.

Mary, Mary

Mary, Mary quite contrary

How does your garden grow?

With silver bells and cockle shells

And pretty maids all in a row!

▸ WHAT TO DO
- Look at the plants in the nursery or garden. Ask the children what they think the plants need in order to grow.
- Introduce the idea of growing sunflowers. Give each child a pot and some compost. Ask them to fill the pot with compost and make a hole with a finger. Show them how to put a seed in the hole and cover it with compost. They can write their name on a label and stick it on their pot. Water the seeds regularly and watch them grow.

9 A garden in miniature

Materials and preparation
- sand tray • small objects to represent different garden elements • pipe-cleaners • model house • miniature people and animals • plates or shallow trays with drainage holes in the bottom • broken clay pots • compost • gravel • pebbles • small plants • moss • plastic cup

 To explore colour, texture, shape and form of different materials

 To use a growing vocabulary to express ideas and convey meaning

👍 Place the different materials in containers so that all the children can reach them easily.

Start this activity by looking at a variety of gardens. Then ask the children to design a garden in the sand tray.

👍 Remember to ask the children to wash their hands after playng with their garden.

Now let the children make a real miniature garden in the shallow bowl.

👍 Choose plants that are easy to look after and that will tolerate the nursery conditions.

1 Place pieces of broken clay pot in the bottom of the bowl to act as drainage.

2 Ask the children to fill the container with compost. Add the plastic cup to form the pond.

3 Let the children choose which plants to use. Ask them to arrange the plants to create the garden.

👍 Fill the plastic cup with coloured water to make it look like real pond water!

4 Help the children to plant the plants. They may like to add furniture and model animals.

OTHER HOMES

Many of the activities in this chapter provide an extension to those contained in chapter one. They are aimed at helping young children to develop their knowledge and understanding of other people's homes. Children are encouraged to participate in a range of activities. Some of the activities focus on exploring features in the local neighbourhood; others make reference to and use stories, songs, rhymes and poems with a strong sense of place.

Activities in this chapter

1
Other homes
A discussion activity to develop children's awareness of the different kinds of home families live in

2
Inside homes
An activity that encourages children to think about the different objects found in homes

3
Make a den
A fun activity providing opportunity for play and discovery

4
Make a house
An activity that encourages children to observe different shapes in the environment so that they can make pictures of different using the shapes they have observed

5
Brick patterns
An activity that encourages children to produce repeating patterns

6
Building houses
Exploratory play is encouraged by turning the sand tray into a building site

7
Unusual homes
Children learn the words and actions to the song, 'There was a Princess Long Ago'

8
Gingerbread house
This activity uses the well-known story Hansel and Gretel as a starting point for making a house and biscuits from gingerbread

9
I'll huff and I'll puff
This activity uses the story The Three Little Pigs to illustrate the strengths of different building materials

10
Piggy storyboard
Children make a large wall frieze using felt elements from the story The Three Little Pigs

1 Other homes

Materials and preparation
- selection of posters and photographs of different homes (flats, houses, bungalows, caravans)

 To talk about where they live

 To show an interest in the experience of others

Questions
- What does your home look like?
- Are there other people's homes nearby?
- Are any of the homes in the pictures alike at all?
- Which home would you like to live in?
- Why would you like to live there?
- What are the homes made of?

This activity uses the children's knowledge as a starting point for talking about the different homes in which people live.

WHAT TO DO
- Collect a selection of photographs and posters of different homes. Use the photographs to make a display. Show the pictures to the children and ask them to think about what they can see.
- Talk about some of the common building materials used in homes.

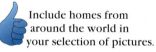 Include homes from around the world in your selection of pictures.

2 Inside homes

Materials and preparation
- a selection of picture books with views of different home interiors • doll's' house and furniture

 To handle objects with appropriate control

 To use mathematical language to describe position

 To explore familiar objects made by humans

 Be sensitive to children's home circumstances.

Use this activity as a starting point for talking about the inside of homes.

WHAT TO DO
- Show the children the different picture books. Invite them to talk about what they can see in the different pictures.
- Introduce the empty doll's house. Ask the children to arrange the furniture in the rooms as they would like it.

Questions
- In which rooms might you find ..?
- Which rooms will you have upstairs?
- Which rooms will you have downstairs?
- Is there anything else you would have liked to have put in the doll's house?

3 Make a den

Making a den provides children with plenty of opportunities to use their imagination while playing.

Materials and preparation
- nursery furniture and equipment, blankets and so on

 To explore and select materials and use building skills

 To show an increasing ability to use imagination and develop pretend scenarios

 To play with other children and solve simple problems with them

 To talk freely with other children. To listen and to observe

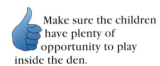 Make sure the children have plenty of opportunity to play inside the den.

▶ WHAT TO DO
- Talk about tents. Ask the children if they have ever been inside one. Perhaps they have a playhouse at home.
- Show the children the blankets and invite them to make their own den.
- Suggest that they use some of the furniture in the nursery.
- Ensure all the children in the nursery have the opportunity to enjoy this activity.

Questions
Before making the den:
- Where will you build your den?
- What can you do in your den?

4 Make a house

Take the children out for a walk in the neighbourhood to look for shapes.

Materials and preparation
- coloured paper triangles, squares, oblongs and so on • paper to mount them on • glue

 To recognise and name a variety of shapes.

 To use appropriate language to describe shape and size

 To explore colour, shape and form in two and three dimensions.

Plan your route in advance so that you can show the children lots of different shapes.

1 Look at different homes in the neighbourhood. Visit a building site. What shapes can the children see on their walk?

2 Ask the children to make pictures of homes using different pieces of coloured paper shapes.

5 Brick patterns

This activity allows children to explore simple repeating and more complex patterns using printing as a technique.

Materials and preparation
- rectangular sponges • mixed powder paint in shallow trays • large sheets of paper on which to print • covered table • overalls for the children to wear

 To explore colour and shape in two dimensions

 To handle tools and objects appropriately and with increasing control

 To recognise and recreate repeating patterns

EXTENSION IDEA
The activity could be made more challenging by introducing a third colour to use in the repeating pattern.

WHAT TO DO
- Take the children outside to look at brick patterns. Talk about the arrangement of bricks.
- Use the sponges to demonstrate how you can print brick shapes. Make a simple repeating pattern, such as blue, red, blue, red. Ask the children if they notice anything about the printing.
- Let the children explore repeating patterns by printing with the sponges.

6 Building houses

Use this activity to give children the opportunity to experiment with different textures and materials.

Materials and preparation
- wooden bricks • house bricks • sand • gravel • other building materials • container in which to mix some sand with water

 To play alongside other children

 To talk freely with other children

 To explore a variety of materials

 Make sure the children understand the importance of using the materials safely.

WHAT TO DO
- Take the children to a building site. Discuss the materials being used.
- Turn the sand tray into a building site. Let the children feel the texture of the bricks, sand and other materials. Mix some sand with water and ask the children to talk about what happens to the sand when it is wet.

EXTENSION IDEA
Turn the outside play area into building site. Give all the children time to explore different materials such as ropes, planks, barrels, logs and off-cuts of tree trunks.

7 Unusual homes

Materials and preparation
- selection of pictures of unusual homes (eg a castle, lighthouse, canal boat, thatched cottage)
- dressing-up props

 To listen and respond to songs

 To show respect for other cultures. To participate in group activities led by an adult

 To enjoy singing and joining in the actions with others

This activity will help children to realise that people can live in all kinds of home.

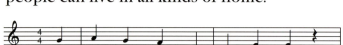
There was a prin-cess long a-go,

Long a go, long a-go. There was a prin-cess

long a go, long a-go.

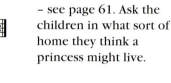

▶ WHAT TO DO
- Show the children the pictures. Ask them if they have seen any homes like these before. Talk about which homes they would like to live in.
- Sing the song shown here (Additional words can be found in 'This Little Puffin' – see page 61. Ask the children in what sort of home they think a princess might live.

☀ EXTENSION IDEA
Let the children dress up as a princess, fairy, bad queen or prince. Teach them some actions for the characters to perform while they sing the song.

---

8 Gingerbread house

Materials and preparation
- gingerbread cutters in the shape of people • raisins • cutting-board • knife • card for the roof

 To understand the importance of hygiene when handling food

 To enjoy listening and responding to stories

 To handle appropriate tools, objects and materials safely and with increasing control

 Make sure the children know how to handle knives and cutters safely so that they do not cut themselves.

This activity is based on the traditional story 'Hansel and Gretel'.

1 Cut the gingerbread into four slices. Cut out windows and a door.

2 Stick the slices together to form the base of the house.

3 Cut out some people from spare gingerbread. Use raisins for the faces.

4 Make the roof of the house from a piece of coloured card.

▶ WHAT TO DO
- Read the story of 'Hansel and Gretel' to the children. Talk about the sweet house. Ask the children why they think it was made of sweets.
- Introduce the idea of making a gingerbread house. The children could have fun making the gingerbread or you could buy it ready made. Follow the step-by-step instructions for making the gingerbread house. Some of the mixture could be used to make gingerbread men and women. Decorate these with raisins and glacé cherries.

9   I'll huff and I'll puff

Materials and preparation
- straw • sticks • bricks • selection of junk materials

 To be aware of mathematical language – first, second and third

 To listen and respond to stories

 To explore different materials

Questions

As you read the story:
- Will the wolf be able to blow this house in?
- What could the pig have done to keep itself safe from the wolf?
- Which material do you think was the best one to use to build a home?

Use the story 'The Three Little Pigs' to help children learn about the strengths of different materials.

WHAT TO DO

- Read the story, emphasising the ordinal aspect of number (first, second and third). Invite the children to make their own homes from junk materials.
- After hearing the story let the children experiment blowing at straw, sticks and bricks.

10   Piggy storyboard

Materials and preparation
- coloured felt for making elements from the story and a background
- felt-tipped pens • Velcro

To make up stories to accompany pictures

To join in group activities led by an adult

This activity can be used as an extension to I'll huff and I'll puff (9).

WHAT TO DO

- Make a storyboard that children can use to retell the story 'The Three Little Pigs'. Cut out pieces of felt to represent the different elements in the story, such as the pigs' houses. Combine different colours of felt and add detail with a felt-tipped pen. Attach Velcro to the back of each piece. Make a felt background on which to stick the felt images.
- Read the story then introduce the storyboard. Let the children take turns to stick an image on the background. Extend the activity by letting the children introduce variations to the story.

PLACES AROUND MY HOME

The focus in this chapter is on learning about places around children's homes. The importance of first-hand experience is emphasised through suggested visits in order to make the most of local features and amenities. The activities assist in heightening the children's interest in their own personal surroundings. Opportunities exist for children to talk about where they live, their local environment and also to show an awareness of the purposes of some features in the area in which they live.

Activities in this chapter

1
My neighbourhood
A directed play activity to develop children's understanding of positional language

2
Tall towers
An activity to explore different materials in order to find out which are good for building

3
Building bridges
This activity uses a popular rhyme as as starting point for looking at bridge shapes, their purpose and construction

4
Bridge shapes
In this activity children are encouraged to work co-operatively in pairs to make bridge shapes with their bodies

5
Photograph puzzles
Jigsaw puzzles made from photographs taken in the local environment are used to encourage skills of observation

6
What's missing?
A memory game that requires children to look carefully at photographs of features in the local environment

7
These people help us
An activity to promote children's language and encourage them to think about people who help in the neighbourhood

8
Make fire-fighters' hats
Step-by-step instructions for making a fire-fighter's hat to be used in role play activities

9
At the doctor's
A role-play activity that encourages children to explore a range of occupations

10
Visiting a post box
Writing a thank you letter leads to a visit to look at a post box in the neighbourhood

1 My neighbourhood

Materials and preparation
- play mat with a road scene or similar
- toy people and vehicles

 To talk about their surroundings

 To use mathematical language to describe position

 To participate in question-and-answer sessions

👍 Develop positional language through questions, for example, 'Where is the ..?', 'What is next to ..?' 'What is in front of ..?'

This activity helps children to think about the different places they visit in their own neighbourhood.

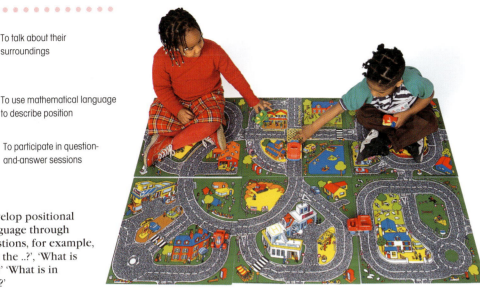

▸ WHAT TO DO
- Ask the children to sit on the floor in a circle. Place the play mat in the middle. Ask the children what they can see on it. Talk about the different amenities. Ask the children which ones they visit in their own neighbourhood. Give the children plenty of opportunity to play with the road scene using the toy people and vehicles.

2 Tall towers

Materials and preparation
- building bricks • different building materials such as Plasticine, Lego, small boxes, tubes, wooden bricks

 To build a tower of five or more bricks and can handle construction materials safely and with increasing control

 To explore different building materials

This activity encourages children to investigate which materials are good for building.

▸ WHAT TO DO
- Take the children outside to look at different buildings. Read 'Miss Brick the Builder's Baby' by Allan Ahlberg and Colin McNaughton. Talk about the different things the baby knocked over.
- Ask the children to use building bricks to build towers. Stress safety by making sure that the towers will not fall on anyone. Remind the children that they should not knock over anybody else's tower.
- Introduce other building materials to the children.

Questions
- Which is the tallest building near the nursery?
- What do you think it is used for?
- What is it made of?

3 Building bridges

Materials and preparation
- pictures of different bridges
- construction materials - card of different strength, art straws and connectors
- different construction sets • adhesive tape • Blu-tak • toy vehicles

 To listen and respond to songs

 To talk about their own environment

 To explore and select materials

 To handle tools and materials safely

 Make sure that experiments involving the children take place at a low level and above a safe surface.

Use the nursery rhyme 'London Bridge is Falling Down' as a starting point for this activity.

London bridge is falling down
London bridge is falling down,
Falling down
London bridge is falling down,
My fair lady.

WHAT TO DO

- Sing 'London Bridge is Falling Down.' Ask the children why they think the bridge is falling down.
- Show the children the pictures. Talk about the purpose of bridges. Think about a bridge nearby. Why was it built? What does it go over?
- Make a bridge outside with planks and boxes.
- Make bridges inside using different materials. Encourage the children to test their bridge by placing objects on it such as a toy vehicle. What happens when you place a toy vehicle on different points of the bridge?

4 Bridge shapes

 To follow simple instructions
To play purposefully with other children

 To move confidently and imaginatively with increasing control and co-ordination

Ask children to make bridge shapes with their bodies, on their own and with a friend.

WHAT TO DO

- Ask the children to make different bridge shapes – high, low, narrow, wide and long. Ask them to find out if a friend can go underneath their bridge.

Always have a high adult–child ratio during physical activities to help prevent accidents.

5 Photograph puzzles

Materials and preparation
- photographs of local features and amenities, for example the shops, the park, the school, the leisure centre, the cinema, the bus or train station cut into several pieces

 To recognise features in their local environment

 To complete simple jigsaw puzzles

This activity can be used as a follow-up to any of the visits around the neighbourhood.

1 For this activity, use photographs taken by the children on previous visits. Cut the photographs into four to six pieces.

Make a duplicate set of photographs so that you can use one set as templates for the children to follow when they are putting the pieces together.

2 Lay the pieces of two photographs in front of the children. Ask them to look at the pieces carefully and then try to put them together to make two pictures. Then try two other pictures.

6 What's missing?

Materials and preparation
- photographs of local features and amenities taken by the children on their outings and visits

 Can recognise features in the local environment

 To take turns in conversation and listen and respond to other children's comments

This version of the traditional game 'Kim's game' is ideal for developing memory skills.

▶ **WHAT TO DO**

- Lay out some photographs of local features, such as a nearby shop, church, park or cinema. Ask the children to look at the pictures for a short while. Discuss and identify each one. Ask one child to turn over one photograph while the other children close their eyes. When he or she shouts 'Ready' the others can open their eyes and must try to work out which picture has been turned over. The first to remember is the next to turn over a photograph. (The photographs can be jumbled between turns.)

EXTENSION IDEA

You could ask the child to turn over two photographs for the others to remember.

7 These people help us

Materials and preparation
- posters depicting people who help us
- appropriate role-play outfits • card to make speech bubbles • marker pen

 To participate in question-and-answer sessions. To talk about pictures and posters

 To talk about the local environment

 To participate in group activities led by an adult

👍 You could use the fire-fighter's hat below in the role play part of this activity.

This activity helps children to recognise that adults are engaged in different occupations.

▶ WHAT TO DO
- Begin by talking about people who help at home and in the nursery. Ask the children to think of the different ways these people help.
- Show the children the pictures. Invite them to say how they think each person helps others. Look at each of the pictures in turn. Ask the children what they think each person might be saying. The children's responses could be recorded in large speech bubbles and displayed with the pictures.
- Let the children dress up as people who help them and ask them to act out appropriate situations.

8 Make fire-fighters' hats

Materials and preparation
- newspaper • balloons • flour and water mixture • scissors • sticky tape • yellow powder paint • paint brushes • silver foil • fire-fighter's hat template

 To explore colour and shape in three dimensions

 To follow simple instructions

 To handle tools and malleable materials with increasing control

 The template for the fire-fighter's helmet can be found on page 63.

Use this fire-fighter's hat for role play activities, acting out stories and when singing songs about fire-fighters.

1 Blow up one balloon for each child. Dip strips of newspaper into the flour and water mixture.

2 Build up layers of newspaper over half the balloon. Allow to dry out. Cut out the peak using the template.

3 Fold the tabs of the peak against the inside of the helmet and secure with sticky tape.

4 Paint the helmet yellow and add a piece of aluminium foil to represent the badge.

▶ WHAT TO DO
- Before starting this activity, find out more about fire-fighters. Visit the local fire station or invite a fire-fighter into the nursery to talk to the children about the job.

9 At the doctor's

This activity encourages children to play imaginatively as part of a group.

Materials and preparation
- boxes or blocks • hospital props eg bandages, doctor's and nurse's uniform, appointment book, signs eg 'Quiet please', posters eg body and eye charts

 To talk freely with other children about their own experiences

 To use events in their life to extend imaginative play

 To play purposefully with other children

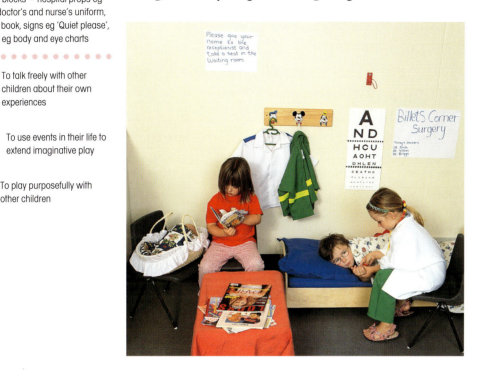

▶ WHAT TO DO
- Begin by asking the children about their own experiences of being in hospital or visiting the doctor. Give them plenty of opportunity to share their thoughts and feelings.
- Introduce the idea of changing the home area into a hospital. Ask the children what they would need. Encourage them to use their imagination and make use of materials already in the nursery. An ambulance and beds can be made from boxes or blocks. Add some real props such as blankets, bandages, a stethoscope, a doctor's coat and a nurse's uniform.

10 Visiting a post box

Write to thank a visitor to the nursery or write to someone that all the children know.

Materials and preparation
- paper • pen • envelope and stamp • range of letters and postcards to start off the activity

 To show awareness of some of the different purposes of writing

 To show an interest in the experiences of others

 To recognise familiar features in the neighbourhood

Encourage children to write their own letters in the nursery area.

▶ WHAT TO DO
- Encourage the children to share their experiences of giving and receiving letters. Introduce the idea of writing a letter to someone. Talk about the person. Ask the children what they would like to say in the letter. Scribe their suggestions. Show the children how to address and stick a stamp on the envelope.

☀ EXTENSION IDEA
Visit the local post box just before collection time. Post the letter in the box. Talk to the postal worker who comes to empty the box.

VISITING THE PARK

The activities in this chapter are all centred around the theme of the park. This is a place that will be familiar to most children. The activities encourage the children to think about the park through group collaboration and creativity and by using stories as a starting point. Children are given many opportunities for investigation through first-hand experience. This enables them to develop their curiosity, to talk about their observations and record them.

Activities in this chapter

1
The park
A visit to the park provides the stimulus for a discussion and book-making activity

2
Fun at the park
The nursery rhyme 'See-saw Margery Daw' is used as a starting point for making see-saws

3
Slides in the park
Children explore a range of materials by making simple slides

4
What makes the best slide?
An investigation that will encourage children to think about which materials allow objects to slide over them easily

5
Where do they live?
A sorting activity which encourages children to consider the habitats of different living things

6
Who lives in the park?
A creative activity in which children make and display their own hedgehogs

7
Bird feeder
This activity gives children an opportunity to care for living creatures in the environment

8
Flying high
Making a kite mobile provides children with an opportunity to explore different colour patterns and helps to develop children's fine motor skills

9
Sounds
Based on two popular picture books, this activity gives children plenty of opportunity to explore sounds associated with the park

10
Similar sounds
Children's awareness and sensitivity to rhyme are developed through the well-known story 'This is the Bear and the Scary Night' by Sarah Hughes.

11
Wild animal picnic
A picnic in the park is the basis for discussing animals and what they eat. It also provides the ideal opportunity for making sandwiches and singing favourite songs

12
Looking at leaf textures
A creative activity that explores the textures of different leaves through rubbings

13
Leaf printing
Printing techniques are explored by using leaves collected by children on their visits to the park

1. The park

Materials and preparation
- home-made book • camera • paper • pencils • coloured crayons • glue • marker pen for writing children's descriptions in the book

 To make up captions to accompany photographs and pictures

 To share their own experiences with others

 To talk about the local environment. To show an awareness of the purposes of some of the things in the neighbourhood

EXTENSION IDEA
Use some of the photographs in activities 5 and 6 in chapter 3.

This activity gives children the opportunity to observe and talk about a familiar place.

▶ **WHAT TO DO**

- Ask the children to tell you about their visits to a park. Talk about what they do in the park – play games, fly kites, feed the ducks, have a picnic, sail model boats etc.
- Visit the local park. Show the children how to use the camera. Let them photograph the different things they see.
- Talk about the park visit and the journey there. Show the children their photographs.
- Introduce the idea of making a class book about the visit. Draw pictures to include in the book. Stick the photographs and drawings into the blank book and ask the children to describe them. Read the book together.

2. Fun at the park

Materials and preparation
- objects of varying weight • small wooden planks or rulers • building blocks • rollers • cotton reels and so on

 To talk about past experiences

 To handle objects safely and with increasing control

 To explore different materials

Questions
- Which rides go up and down/backwards and forwards etc?
- Do you like riding a see-saw with a big or small person? Why?

Use this activity as a follow-up to playing in a park play area.

See-Saw Margery Daw

See-Saw Margery Daw,

Johnny shall have a new master,

He shall have but a penny a day,

Because he can't work any faster.

▶ **WHAT TO DO**

- Talk about the visit to the park. Ask the children to tell you about their favourite play equipment.
- Recite the nursery rhyme 'See-saw Margery Daw'. Introduce the idea of making see-saws from lengths of wood and building blocks. Talk about the up-and-down action of a see-saw.
- Let the children place different objects at either end of their see-saws. Talk about what happens.

3 Slides in the park

Materials and preparation
- planks of wood • building bricks
- teddy bears and other cuddly toys

 To use a range of small and large equipment with increasing skill. To move confidently and imaginatively on large climbing apparatus

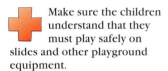 To explore materials and talk about their observations

Make sure the children understand that they must play safely on slides and other playground equipment.

In this activity children design a simple slide for their toys.

WHAT TO DO
- Give the children plenty of opportunity to use the nursery slide. Explore the different ways of travelling down it.
- Ask the children to make their own slides using planks of wood and building bricks. Let them slide teddy bears and other cuddly toys down the slides. Ask the children if they think their slides are safe.
- Talk about other things that slide, such as sledges and skis.

4 What makes the best slide?

Materials and preparation
- planks of wood covered in different materials (some smooth, rough, shiny, bumpy, etc.) • building bricks
- cuddly toys

 To handle materials safely and with increasing control

 To make predictions. To explore materials and express concepts such as rough and smooth

EXTENSION IDEA
Take the children to different slides in the neighbourhood to find out which one is best. Talk about why it is best.

This activity can form a follow-up to 'Slides in the park' (3).

1 Prop up each piece of board on a building brick to make a slide. Make some slides very steep and others not so steep.

WHAT TO DO
- Ask the children to feel the planks covered in different materials. Talk about what each surface feels like.
- Let the children make slides with the planks and building blocks. Encourage them to slide their cuddly toys down the slides. Talk about which slide is best.

2 Place a cuddly toy at the top of one slide. Watch it slide down. Place it on a second slide.

3 Let the children experiment placing the toys in different positions on the slides.

4 Ask the children to experiment with the different surfaces. Record their observations.

5 Where do they live?

Materials and preparation
- three sorting rings • picture cards of different animals

To recognise living things in the environment

To sort things into sets

This activity allows children to learn how to sort things according to set criteria.

▶ **WHAT TO DO**
- Read 'Tales from Percy's Park' by Nick Butterworth. Ask the children to tell you which animals Percy might see in the park.
- Show the children the cards, one at a time. Ask them if they think the creature lives mainly on land, in water or air.
- Ask the children to place the card into the appropriate sorting ring.
- Some creatures, for example a frog, will belong in more than one ring. Make sure you give the children the chance to discuss this.

EXTENSION IDEA

Visit the local park or nursery garden. Take magnifying glasses through which the children can observe small creatures. Find out where creatures live by looking in different parts of the park.

6 Who lives in the park?

Materials and preparation
- pictures of hedgehogs • self-hardening clay or another modelling material e.g. Plasticine • paint • art straws

 To recognise features of living things

 To handle tools, objects and materials appropriately and with increasing control

 To explore colour, texture, shape and form in two and three dimensions

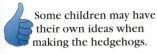 Some children may have their own ideas when making the hedgehogs.

Children will enjoy making these hedgehogs.

▶ **WHAT TO DO**
- Show the children the hedgehog pictures. Talk about the distinctive parts of a hedgehog – eg its snout and prickles.
- Ask the children to roll clay into a ball and add a snout. Cut the art straws and let the children push them into the clay for prickles. Paint the hedgehogs and display them when they are dry.

Questions
- Where do hedgehogs live?
- Have you ever seen a hedgehog?
- What do hedgehogs do if they are frightened?

7 Bird feeder

Materials and preparation
- coconut • knife • string • bird seed and melted fat

To concentrate for a reasonable amount of time
To learn to treat living things with care and concern

To explore materials
To observe living things and to explore patterns and change
To talk about their observations

Place the bird feeder where it can be seen from the nursery window.

This activity encourages children to care for wild animals.

1 In advance, remove the white flesh from the coconut. Make two holes as shown above.

2 Attach string to the coconut through the holes so that you can hang the bird feeder outside.

3 Mix the bird seed with the melted fat. Pack this into the coconut and leave it to set. Hang the coconut upside down for the birds.

8 Flying high

Materials and preparation
- square base boards of stiff card
- red and blue triangles that cover one quarter of a base • string, thread, ribbon or crepe of different colours • glue

To use mathematical language to describe shape, position, size and quantity

To handle tools appropriately and with increasing control

To explore materials and look closely at similarities and differences

This activity can be done in conjuction with 'Finding out about the wind' (13) page 61.

Questions
- How many green/yellow triangles have you used?
- Which kite has the longest tail?
- Which kite has the shortest tail?
- How many bows/ribbons are on your kite?

1 Rule lines from corner to corner across the boards. Ask the children to choose four triangles. Stick them in place.

2 Attach string to one corner of the kites for a tail. Decorate the tails with ribbons. Attach a length of thread to the opposite corner of the kites with which to hold them.

3 Take the kites outside to see how they move in the breeze.

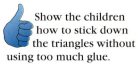
Show the children how to stick down the triangles without using too much glue.

EXTENSION IDEA
After taking the kites outside, hang them as mobiles from the nursery ceiling. Encourage the children to discuss the different arrangements of triangles.

9 Sounds

Materials and preparation
- cassette player and tape of outdoor sounds • pictures relating to the sounds

 To listen and respond to stories

 To know that sounds can be made in lots of different ways

 To show an increasing ability to use imagination by creating stories about a sound

This activity encourages children to communicate and to express their ideas and feelings in a creative way.

▶ WHAT TO DO
- Read 'In the Small, Small Pond' or 'In the Tall Tall Grass' both by Denise Fleming. Talk about the noises in the story and let the children try making them.
- Ask the children what sounds they think they might hear in a park, for example, children laughing, people talking, ducks quacking, leaves rustling.
- Play a tape of outdoor sounds while the children look at the picture cards showing the things that make the sounds. Ask them to pick out the correct picture as they listen to each sound.

EXTENSION IDEA
Let the children fill small tins and boxes with rice, lentils, buttons and so on. Ask them to shake the tins and describe the sound.

10 Similar sounds

 To listen attentively. To begin to associate sounds with patterns in rhymes

This activity is intended to develop children's awareness of rhyme.

👍 Help the children to notice the rhyming words by emphasising them the first time you read the story.

▶ WHAT TO DO
- Read the story 'This is the Bear and the Scary Night' (see resources). Ask the children if they notice anything about some of the words. Say two of the rhyming words. Read the story again, see if the children can supply the second rhyming word.

EXTENSION IDEAS
Play rhyming I spy: 'I spy with my little eye, something in the book that rhymes with dark' (park).
- See if the children can find rhyming words in familiar nursery rhymes.
- Try playing the following game. Ask the children to add a rhyme – I went to the shops and I bought a rat, a cat and a ... ?

37

11 Wild animal picnic

Materials and preparation
• bread • butter or margarine • blunt knife • sandwich fillings • animal-shape cutters • drinks • picnic blanket

 To participate in group activities led by an adult

 To show an understanding of the importance of hygiene when handling food

 To show an understanding of the different purposes of writing

 To match objects 1:1

✹ EXTENSION IDEAS
- Teach the children the song 'The Teddy Bears' Picnic'.
- Make invitations to send out. Guests could include family members and people who help the children, such as the lollypop person.

▶ WHAT TO DO
- Collect different sorts of vegetation that animals familar to the children would eat, eg nuts, fruit, leaves and berries.
- Ask the children to bring in their toy mice, rabbits, hedgehogs, birds, and other small animals. Make a display using the vegetation and the toys.
- Use the display to prompt a discussion with the children about what different animals eat. You could do this as a follow-up to the picnic or on a wet day when you cannot go out to the park.

Children make animal-shape sandwiches and plan a picnic in the park.

After the picnic talk to the children about the different kinds of food wild animals found in the park may eat.

▶ WHAT TO DO
- Discuss with the children what a picnic is. Talk about picnics they have had. Ask them where they went on a picnic.
- Introduce the idea of having a picnic in the park. Make preparations for the picnic with the children. Make a list of guests, food, songs you will sing and games you will play. Discuss which wild animals might be in the park, such as rabbits. Make sandwiches shaped like the animals. Show the children how to place one piece directly on top of another.
- Hold the picnic. Sing the songs and play the games chosen by the children.

Questions
- What is the best kind of weather for a picnic?
- How will we carry the food for the picnic?

✚ Make sure the children understand they must not eat wild berries and plants because they may be poisonous.

38

12 Looking at leaf textures

Materials and preparation
- paper • thick wax crayons • powder paint mixed very thinly • paint brushes • a selection of different leaves collected by the children

 To talk about their observations

 To explore texture, shape and form

Children explore the texture of different leaves and make rubbings.

When making the rubbings, use Blu-tak to keep the paper still.

WHAT TO DO
- Ask the children to feel one of their leaves carefully. Encourage them to close their eyes when they are doing this.
- Talk about the textures, introducing appropriate language such as smooth, rough, bendy, firm.
- Show the children how to make a rubbing of a leaf. Place a piece of paper on top of the leaf. Hold the paper steady and rub over the top of the paper with a wax crayon. Fill the paper with rubbings of different leaves.
- Ask the children to paint over the rubbings gently. Watch what happens.

13 Leaf printing

Materials and preparation
- newspaper • paper • powder or poster paint • brushes • a selection of leaves collected by the children

 To handle tools appropriately and with increasing control

 To explore colour, texture and shape

This activity can be done as a follow-up to a park visit.

Give each child a thick wad of newspaper to act as a base when they are printing. This will help them to make clearer prints.

WHAT TO DO
- Ask the children to paint one side of a leaf ensuring they don't put the paint on too thickly. Show them how to press their leaf down carefully on to the paper. Help them peel the leaf away from the paper. Encourage the children to make prints with other leaves.
- Ask the children to try printing with both sides of a leaf. Does it make a difference? Do some leaves print better than others?
- Talk about the different shapes and patterns the children have made with their leaf prints.

A VISIT TO THE SHOPS

In this chapter children are encouraged to think about shops in their neighbourhood and the services they provide. Children should be given opportunities to talk about their own experiences of shopping. The activities in this chapter should be supported by visits to the local shops and plenty of role play. This could include setting up different kinds of shop and restaurant. Some of the activities encourage sorting objects according to attributes suggested by the children themselves.

Activities in this chapter

1
I went to the shops and bought
A memory game that encourages children to take turns and so develop social skills

2
Eating out
A role play activity that encourages children to play together, developing their language and social skills

3
The baker's shop
Children's knowledge of number is developed by learning a popular song based on a backery

4
Being a baker
A follow-up to 'The Baker's shop' in which children play with salt dough and make imitation bread rolls

5
Which shop?
An activity to encourage children to think about the different kinds of shos in their own neighbourhood

6
Packaging
In this activity children use packaging to explore materials and shapes

7
Round or long?
This sorting activity develops and extends children's mathematical thinking and concludes by making a fruit salad

8
Heavy or light?
A practical activity that encourages children to think about the relative weights of different objects bought from a supermarket

9
Shopping lists
A well-known picture book story provides the starting point for children to make their own shopping lists

10
Shopping bags
An activity to investigate the usefulness of bags for carrying shopping

1 I went to the shops and bought

 To listen attentively

 To take turns

TIP Have some shopping items for the children to choose from in the middle of the circle. Children will then have a visual reference. As the game proceeds, the children can think of their own items.

This activity is a game that children will enjoy playing, and is a useful activity for developing their memory skills.

▶ WHAT TO DO

- Arrange the children in a circle to play the game. One child begins by saying, 'I went to the shops and I bought a ...' and names an item. The next child repeats the sentence, adding an item, and so on.

2 Eating out

Materials and preparation

• aprons • cutlery • chairs • table
• writing materials for making a menu and taking orders • white crêpe paper and card • glue • tape

To use events in their own life as a starting point for imaginative play

To understand writing has different purposes and to pretend read menus etc.

To play purposefully with other children

Dining out is a popular pastime that children love to role play.

▶ WHAT TO DO

- Talk to the children about times they have eaten out.
- Introduce the idea of turning one area of the nursery into a café or restaurant. Ask the children to suggest which items they will need. Show the children how to set the table. Let them choose which roles they would like to play.
- Follow the steps for making a chef's hat.

1 Roll up the crêpe paper and gather one end together with tape.

2 Cut the base from card, to fit the child's head. Attach inside the crêpe.

3 The baker's shop

Materials and preparation
- five 1p coins • five currant buns as props for the song

 To talk about familiar places, such as shops

 To become familiar with number rhymes

 To listen and respond to rhymes

Children will develop an awareness of number by learning and singing this rhyme.

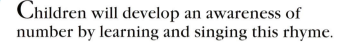
Five cur-rant buns in a ba-ker's shop,

Round and fat with a cher-ry on the top. A-

long came a boy with a pen-ny one day,

Bought a cur-rant bun and took it right a-way.

▶ WHAT TO DO
- Talk about the baker's shop. Ask the children if they know what else the baker sells apart from bread.
- Teach the children the song 'Five Currant Buns in the Baker's Shop'. Encourage them to act out the song using the currant buns and coins to help them.

Where the song says 'a boy' replace it with the child's name.

4 Being a baker

Materials and preparation
- real bread rolls as examples
- 1 mug of flour • 1/2 mug of salt
- 1 teaspoon of cooking oil • 1 mug of water • food colouring (optional)
- bread board

 To explore materials and equipment

To use a range of materials and tools

 To use appropriate mathematical language to talk about size and quantity

Use salt dough to make imitation food.

1 Give the children a ball of dough each.

2 Encourage them to play with the dough.

▶ WHAT TO DO
- Make the dough by mixing all the ingredients together in a pan over a low heat. Stir the mixture with a wooden spoon until it becomes solid. Tip the mixture out of the pan and knead it well until it is cool and smooth.

3 Show the children some real bread rolls and other items that can be bought at the baker's shop. Encourage them to copy the shapes with their dough.

 Make real bread-making a regular activity in the nursery. Let all the children have a turn at kneading the dough.

☀ EXTENSION IDEA
Use the items the children make in other role-play activities.

5 Which shop?

Materials and preparation
- a shopping basket or bag containing items from different shops, such as food, clothing, toys, toiletries

 To participate in group activities led by an adult

 To talk about their environment

 To participate in question-and-answer sessions

This activity can be a starting point for talking about shops in the neighbourhood.

1 Remove one item from the shopping basket. Show it to the children and ask them to identify it. Ask them at what sort of shop you bought it.

2 Talk about all the items in the shopping basket one at a time.

3 Ask the children to group together items that you bought from the same shop.

Make sure you have a variety of items to talk about.

Questions
- What other things might you buy from the baker/newsagent etc?
- Do you like going to the supermarket?
- Why?

6 Packaging

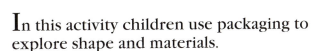

Materials and preparation
- a large collection of packages and containers

 To handle tools and objects appropriately

 To count, name and recognise shapes

 To explore materials

In this activity children use packaging to explore shape and materials.

▶ WHAT TO DO
- Collect a range of packets. Talk about the different shapes. Ask the children to stack the packets on top of each other. See how tall they can stack them. Do some packages stack better than others? Look at the lettering on the packaging. Do the children recognise any of the words or letters?

Ask the children to bring in some empty packages from home.

 EXTENSION IDEA
Show the children how to unfold some empty packages. Look at the different shapes of card that make the packages. Count the number of rectangles, circles, etc.

7 Round or long?

Materials and preparation
- selection of round and long fruit and vegetables • tablecloth and sorting rings or hoops • chopping boards • plastic knives • large bowl • individual bowls and spoons

 To look closely at similarities and differences. To understand the importance of hygiene when handling food

 To sort everyday objects using their own criteria

Questions
- Which is your favourite fruit/vegetable?
- Can you taste the different fruit in the fruit salad?
- What other fruit could you put in the salad?

This activity encourages children to make up their own reasons for grouping objects.

 If you let the children chop up the fruit and vegetables, ensure they are closely supervised.

▶ **WHAT TO DO**
- Ask the children to identify and describe the fruit and vegetables. Ask them to group together the round fruit and vegetables and the long ones.
- Invite them to think of other ways to group the fruit and vegetables for example heavy/light or by colour.
- Introduce the idea of making fruit salad. Let each child help to chop the fruit. Mix the fruit with some orange juice. Provide each child with a spoon and bowl and divide the fruit salad amongst them. Encourage the children to describe its flavour.

8 Heavy or light?

Materials and preparation
- about four supermarket items of different weights

 To use mathematical language to describe measure

Questions
- Which things do you think are heavy/light?
- Is the washing up liquid heavier than the lettuce?
- Are the tea bags heavier than the cat food?
- Which is the heaviest item?
- Which is the lightest item?

This activity encourages children to think about relative weights.

▶ **WHAT TO DO**
- Put our all the materials on the table. Invite the children to pick up the materials in turn. Name the objects and introduce comparative language, such as lighter than and heavier than. Ask one child to pick up a named item and say if it feels heavy or light. Pass the item around each child in turn. Compare it with another item. Let each child hold the two items, one in each hand. Invite them to say again which is the lightest. Repeat the process for the other items. Invite the children to arrange the items in order of weight.

9 Shopping lists

Materials and preparation
- an example of a shopping list
- long strips of paper for shopping lists
- colouring pencils or felt-tipped pens
- items to sell at a shop (optional)

 To talk about familiar places

To listen and respond to stories.
To understand that writing has different purposes.
To use pictures, symbols, familiar words and letters in their emergent writing

Questions
- What would you like to buy at the shops? Why?
- How many items are on your list?

Use 'Don't Forget the Bacon' by Pat Hutchins as a starting point for this activity.

▶ **WHAT TO DO**
- Read the story (see resources for more information).
- Ask the children to say why they think people write shopping lists. Show them a shopping list you have made. Read the list out to the children.
- Show the children the long strips of paper and invite them to write their own lists. Some children may prefer to draw items. Look at the children's lists with them. Talk about in which shops they would find the different items.

👍 Set up a shop. Ask the children to write a shopping list before visiting it.

10 Shopping bags

Materials and preparation
- an assortment of empty packets

 To talk about past experiences

 To listen and respond to rhymes

Use the rhyme 'Baa Baa Black Sheep' as a focus for discussing how useful bags are.

Baa, Baa, Black Sheep

Baa, baa, black sheep

Have you any wool?

Yes, sir, yes, sir, three bags full.

One for the master,

And one for the dame,

And one for the little boy

Who lives down the lane.

▶ **WHAT TO DO**
- Recite the nursery rhyme 'Baa Baa Black Sheep'. Encourage the children to join in. Ask the children who the three bags were for. What did the bags have inside them?
- Talk about the children's experiences of shopping. Ask them what they think it would be like if people had to carry shopping home without a bag.
- Let the children try carrying an assortment of empty packages. How difficult is it? How many can they carry before they drop one?
- Ask the children to tell you about other kinds of bag and what they are used for.

JOURNEYS

The activities in this chapter encourage children to think about the different journeys they make in their neighbourhood. These journeys may be to friends and family, the local shops or to amenities such as the park, cinema or leisure centre. The activities will encourage children to develop their understanding through first-hand experience. Included are activities in the form of discussions, games, songs and rhymes, role play and acting.

Activities in this chapter

1
Traffic watching
A discussion activity to consider the different kinds of transport

2
People carriers
An activity to encourage children to think about the number of people who can travel inside the different forms of transport

3
Trains, boats and aeroplanes
A game that encourages children to listen carefully and respond to the teacher's instructions

4
All aboard
Using nursery furniture to make a bus

5
The wheels on the bus
An extension to 'All aboard', in which children sing 'The Wheels on the Bus' while miming the actions

6
Here comes the bus
Using a number rhyme to develop children's awareness of number operations based on their existing knowledge and understanding

7
Little Red Riding Hood
An opportunity to dress up and act out a well-known story

8
Traffic lights game
A game to encourage children to listen carefully to instructions

9
Traffic lights pattern
Producing repeated patterns through a printing activity

10
Finding your way
An activity to consider the different wayss of getting from one place to another

11
Make a story map
Children make a story map based on the story 'The Three Little Pigs'

12
Words everywhere
The importance and function of print in the local environment is considered in this activity

13
Travel agents
Setting up a travel agents provides the opportunity to talk about journeys beyond the children's immediate environment

1 Traffic watching

Materials and preparation
- a selection of different model trains, planes, boats and other vehicles

 To talk about past and present events in their own lives

 To talk about own experiences in a small group

Take the children on a walk near the nursery to see different types of transport.

Ask the children to bring in some model vehicles. Make a display with the models when you have finished the activity.

WHAT TO DO
- Talk about the different types of transport the children saw on their walk. Ask them if they can think of any more.
- Talk about the children's journeys to and from nursery.
- Collect a selection of model boats, cars, trains etc. Talk about how the models are different from the real things. Ask the children how they think the models work.

Questions
- What do the different forms of transport carry?
- Which moves the fastest?
- Where would you go to catch a train?
- Have you ever been on an aeroplane?
- Where did you go?

2 People carriers

Materials and preparation
- selection of posters and pictures of different forms of transport
- model cars, planes and so on

 To participate in question-and-answer sessions

 To participate in group activities led by an adult

 To show mathematical awareness in other areas of learning

This activity gives children an opportunity to talk about their travel experiences.

Include animals in your selection of forms of transport, such as a horse and camel.

WHAT TO DO
- Show the children the pictures and models of different forms of transport.
- Ask the children to tell you about their own experiences of travelling.
- Ask them to think about how many people each form of transport can carry.

EXTENSION IDEAS
Organise a trip to a bus station so that the children can see a variety of buses. Arrange for them to go on a bus and count the number of seats.

3 Trains, boats and aeroplanes

 To move confidently with increasing control and co-ordination with awareness of space and others

 To follow simple instructions

This circle game will generate considerable excitement – watch out for bumps and falls.

This game encourages children to participate in a group activity.

▶ WHAT TO DO
- Sit the children in a circle. Before playing the game, go around the circle, touching each child and telling them whether they are a 'boat', 'train' or 'plane'.

▶ GAME RULES
- Tell the children that when you call out 'Boats', all the boats change places. When you call out 'Trains', then all the trains change. When you call out 'Transport', then they all have to change places.

4 All aboard

Materials and preparation
- nursery furniture with which to make a bus
- card, paint and brushes for making a bus stop

 To play purposefully alongside other children

 To use a growing vocabulary to communicate ideas

 To use their imagination with increasing ability during role-play activities

This role play activity will encourage children to share their own experiences with other children.

▶ WHAT TO DO
- Visit a bus stop to watch the buses arrive and depart.
- Introduce the idea of making a bus and bus stop for the nursery. Use nursery furniture to make the bus. Add the destination to the front of the bus. Make and display a bus stop sign.

Encourage the children in their role play by suggesting real life situations, such as paying a fare and losing a ticket.

5 The wheels on the bus

 To take turns

 To listen and respond to songs

Use the bus that the children made in the previous activity.

1. The wheels on the bus go round and round,

Round and round, round and round. The

wheels on the bus go round and round.

All day long.

WHAT TO DO

- Sing, 'The Wheels on the Bus' and mime the actions. (The four verses are given below.)
- Let the children take it in turns to be the driver who holds a cardboard steering wheel.
- Create additional verses for other passengers.

1. The wheels on the bus go round and round
2. The mummies on the bus go nod nod nod
3. The babies on the bus go waa waa waa
4. The daddies on the bus go chatter chatter chatter

6 Here comes the bus

Materials and preparation
- chairs arranged in the shape of a bus
- picture of a double-decker bus

 To recite number rhymes. To show an awareness of number operations

To listen and respond to rhymes

This activity provides an opportunity for the children to use the bus they have made.

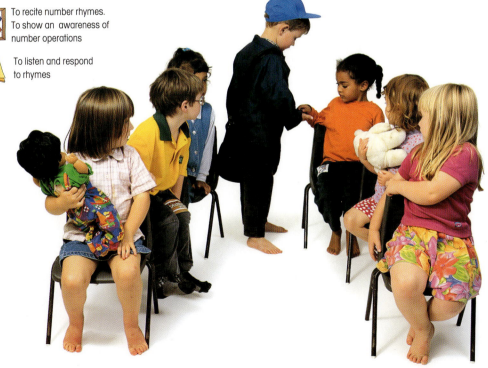

WHAT TO DO

- Talk about the different kinds of bus. Show the children a picture of a double-decker bus. Ask them why they think it has an upstairs.
- Teach the children the following number rhyme:
  Here comes the bus,
  It's going to stop.
  In you pop.
  Four inside and six on top.
- Act out the rhyme. Insert different numbers of passengers, according to the children's awareness and understanding of number.
- Ask questions such as 'If there are two children inside and one on top, how many are there altogether?'

7 Little Red Riding Hood

Materials and preparation
- appropriate story props, for example, a basket with a gift for a poorly grandparent • a headband with wolf ears attached and a red cape

 To show through stories and imaginative play an increasing ability to use their imagination, to listen and to observe

 To listen and respond to stories

 To participate in group activities led by an adult

Use the story of 'Little Red Riding Hood' for role play and as a starting point for talking about personal safety.

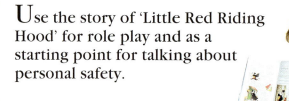

▶ WHAT TO DO
- Retell the traditional story 'Little Red Riding Hood'.
- Ask questions such as, How do you think Red Riding Hood knew which way to go? Who did she meet on the way? Do you think she was right to speak to the wolf?
- Help the children to act out the first part of the story.
- Talk about what you can do if you are lost. Who should you talk to? Who could help you?

8 Traffic lights game

Materials and preparation
- traffic light made from a cereal box painted black and three cardboard circles represening a red, amber and green light

 To follow simple instructions

 To listen and respond when others are speaking

This activity reinforces the need to listen to instructions carefully.

▶ WHAT TO DO
- Show the children the traffic light and discuss what the coloured discs tell you.
- Explain that you are going to play a variation on the traditional traffic lights game. Explain the rules and then put the discs on the traffic light in turn.

☀ GAME RULES
- The green disc means put your hands in the air.
- The amber disc means fold your arms.
- The red disc means put your hands behind your back.

9 Traffic lights pattern

Materials and preparation
- paper • mixed powder paints (red, orange and green) in shallow trays
- circular objects for printing, for example cotton reels, a potato cut in half and circular sponges

 To handle tools and objects with increasing control

Provide a different sponge for each colour. Try using a variety of round objects to print the three colours.

Children will enjoy making patterns based on the traffic lights sequence.

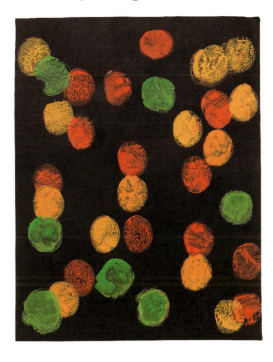

WHAT TO DO

- Take the children to look at a set of traffic lights. Observe the sequence of colours for traffic lights. Ask the children what happens when the lights are red. What happens when the lights are green?
- Introduce the idea of making repeating patterns to show the sequence of lights. Make a red circular print. Ask the children what colour comes next. Print the colour and ask the question again. Repeat the process as necessary.
- Let the children make their own repeating patterns.

10 Finding your way

Materials and preparation
- small toy vehicle • road playmat

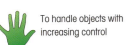 To handle objects with increasing control

Questions
- Where is the park?
- Can you find the school?
- How would you get from the school to the hospital?
- Could you go another way?

Introduce this activity by encouraging the children to play with a road scence play mat to familiarise themselves with its features.

 To participate in group activities led by an adult

 To show an understanding of directions and routes

WHAT TO DO

- Ask the children to find specific points on the playmat. Talk about the features the children find.
- Ask the children to take a toy vehicle on a journey from one feature to another.
- Ask the children to work in pairs. One child could name two features while the other makes the journey.

11 Make a story map

Materials and preparation
- a variety of materials to make the pigs' houses • large sheet of paper
- felt-tipped pens

 To name familiar features, such as shops, parks, woods, farms

 To use skills such as cutting, joining, folding and building

 To use a widening range of materials to express ideas

Make a story map based on the story of 'The Three Little Pigs'.

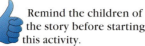 Remind the children of the story before starting this activity.

▶ WHAT TO DO
- Make models of the pigs' houses. These could be made from cereal boxes painted and covered in appropriate materials. Place the houses on a large sheet of paper.
- Ask questions such as, How would each pig visit the others? Where do you think the pigs got their food from? Draw on pathways and roads and add an orchard, shops or a farm, depending on the children's suggestions.
- Add other features such as fields, a park, etc.
- Encourage the children to retell the story in their own words using the story map.

12 Words everywhere

Materials and preparation
- camera • examples of writing in the neighbourhood

 To talk about their environment

 To know that words and pictures carry meaning. To recognise some familiar words.

 To recognise letters of the alphabet. To be aware of the different purposes of writing

Children examine different words in the local environment.

▶ WHAT TO DO
- Take the children for a walk near the nursery. Ask them to take photographs of the different writing they see including road names, shop fronts, posters, etc. Photograph the nursery's name sign, too.
- Ask the children to think about why the writing is there. Talk about why they think it is written there.
- Make a display of the children's photographs and other examples of writing found in the environment.

Be well prepared for the walk and know where the children can find some interesting writing.

13 Travel agents

Materials and preparation
- travel brochures
- posters of various destinations
- props for a travel agent's eg a telephone, booking forms, pens
- card to make luggage labels
- string
- marker pens

 To know that people make journeys for different reasons

 To talk about events in their own life and use such experiences to extend imaginative play. To play as part of a group

 To listen and respond to stories

Questions
- Where would you go to find information about going on holiday?
- Have you been on holiday?
- Where did you go?
- How did you get there?

Set up a travel agent's to find out more about places beyond the children's neighbourhood.

WHAT TO DO
- Visit a travel agent's to find out what the people working there do and what the inside of the shop looks like.
- Talk about holidays the children have been on.
- Introduce the idea of changing the home corner into a travel agent's. Assign children different roles, such as customer and assistant, making sure children have an opportunity to change roles on another occasion if they want to.
- Spend time using the role play area with the children. Take on the role of a customer yourself.

 Use as many real props as possible.

Extend the activity by making luggage labels.

1 Show the children a suitcase with a luggage label attached. Read the label to the children and explain why it is used.

Let the children tie their label on their bag or case.

2 Introduce the idea of making labels. Show the children the card and string. Ask them to write their name on a label.

3 Look at different countries on a globe. Ask the children to choose destinations to write on their luggage labels.

OUT AND ABOUT

There is a selection of general activities in this chapter. The activities will encourage children to think about their neighbourhood through group discussion, role play and by creating things. Some of the activities are designed to develop children's understanding of the weather and how changes in it affect our everyday lives. To reinforce children's understanding of the weather, many activities include rhymes and songs about the weather.

Activities in this chapter

1
Which comes first?
An activity that uses story cards to develop children's skills at putting things in sequence

2
Blind man's buff
This activity aims to make children aware of the difficulties that blind or partially blind people have

3
Our friends
An activity to consider the importance of friendship and things children like to do with their friends

4
Helping each other
An activity that welcomes newcomers into the nursery

5
Special clothes
A game that encourages close observation and awareness of the clothes people wear for different jobs

6
Posting letters
A creative activity in which the children make a postbox. This is then used to encourage correspondence within the class

7
Weather
A song is used to stimulate talk about the weather

8
Rainy days
A discussion about the need for wet-weather clothes

9
Keeping dry
This interactive activity shows children how to protect themselves from the rain

10
Is it waterproof?
An investigation to find out how waterproof different fabrics are

11
Keeping cool
This introduces children to the importance of protecting themselves from the sun

12
Which clothes?
An activity to establish how the weather influences our decisions as to what clothes to wear

13
Finding out about the wind
An activity to do outside on a windy day

14
I can see a rainbow
This activity uses a popular song as a stimulus for making rainbow patterns

1 Which comes first?

Materials and preparation
- a sequence of story cards (photocopy the colour illustrations in 'Tom and Pippo go for a Walk' by Helen Oxenbury)

 To use mathematical language – first, second, third, next, last

 To follow a sequence and make up stories to accompany pictures

TIPS
- Cover the cards with clear self-adhesive film so that they will last longer for use on other occasions.
- Let the children record their stories on tape.
- Write down the children's stories in a book for keeping in the reading corner.

This activity encourages children to think about the order in which events happen.

WHAT TO DO
- Show the children one of the sequencing picture cards. Ask the children to tell you what they think is happening in the picture. Place the card in front of the children and repeat the process with all the other cards.
- Ask the children to put the cards in the order in which they think the events happened. Invite them to make up their own story using this arrangement of cards.

2 Blind man's buff

Materials and preparation
- a scarf large enough to use as a blindfold

 To walk along a path or course. To control body movements in order to stand still and reach down

 To be sensitive to the needs of others. To follow simple instructions

Questions
- To a blindfolded child: In which direction is the door/window/cupboard?
- What do you think would be useful to help you find your way?

This game encourages children to listen carefully and follow instructions.

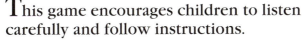

Supervise this activity carefully and be sensitive to children who may be afraid of being blindfolded.

Invite a blind person into the nursery to talk to the children and give a positive perspective.

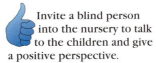

WHAT TO DO
- Ask a child to collect a specific object. Repeat the exercise but this time blindfold the child. Stay close to the child to prevent any accidents. Ask why it was more difficult the second time.
- Play blind man's buff (a blindfolded child tries to find the others). Let one child give the blindfolded child verbal instructions. Give each child a turn at being blindfolded.
- Ask the children to think about how they can tell where they are (by touch, counting steps, listening to familiar sounds, etc).
- Ask the children to think about how a blind person finds their way around.

3 Our friends

Materials and preparation
- pieces of rectangular paper
- coloured and ordinary pencils
- dark coloured paper on which to mount children's pictures

 To control a pencil to draw a person

Questions
- What do you like to play with your friends?
- Do you visit each other's houses?
- Where else do you play together?

Make a friendship wall with the children.

 To show an interest in other children and in forming friendships

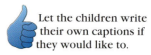 Let the children write their own captions if they would like to.

▶ **WHAT TO DO**
- Talk to the children about the different things they like to do with their friends. Invite them to tell you about what they enjoy doing at nursery.
- Ask the children to draw a picture of themselves playing with a friend. Add captions by writing down the children's comments.
- Write the children's names very clearly underneath the pictures so that they can be read from a distance.
- Make a wall display of the pictures by arranging them in a brickwork pattern. Mount them on a dark background.

4 Helping each other

Materials and preparation
- card • safety pins • felt-tipped pens

 To be sensitive to the needs and feelings of others. Is confident in a new environment/situation. Can participate in group activities led by an adult

 To listen and respond to stories

EXTENSION IDEA
Group the children into pairs to make name badges. Each child can make and decorate a badge for their partner.

Use this activity to help newcomers to the nursery to feel welcome and to encourage children's awareness of the feelings of others.

 Some children may prefer to tell you what they like doing at nursery.

▶ **WHAT TO DO**
- Read Starting School by Janet and Allan Ahlberg or Going to Playschool by Sarah Garland.
- Ask the children to sit in a circle. Include yourself in the circle.
- Go round the circle asking each child to say their name. Go round the circle again but this time ask the children to finish the sentence, 'Something I enjoy doing is ...' Do it yourself to start them off.

5 Special clothes

This activity encourages children to make predictions.

Materials and preparation
- sample uniform from the dressing-up box • puzzles depicting people wearing uniforms (or selection of photographs of people in uniform, which you can reveal bit by bit)

To know that adults do different kinds of work

To participate in question-and-answer sessions

To talk about their observations

Questions
- Why do some people wear special clothes.
- Why do you think it is the traffic warden/doctor/nurse?
- How did you know it was the postperson, painter? (eg colour of uniform, material, hat, badge etc)

WHAT TO DO
- Talk about people who wear special clothes or uniforms for their jobs. Use items from the dressing-up box.
- Show the children the puzzles. Explain that the pictures are of people in different uniforms. Give the children time to play with them and familiarise themselves with the uniforms.
- Give the children one piece of puzzle at a time. Encourage them to say which uniform they think it is. Give them more pieces, one at a time, encouraging them each time to predict which uniform it is.

6 Posting letters

Ask the children to write to each other. Make a postbox so they can post the letters.

Materials and preparation
- large piece of corrugated card painted red • strong red card • scissors • glue or sticky tape • paper and envelopes • pens and pencils

 To use mathematical language to describe shape

 To show an interest in other children

1 Cut a slot in the corrugated card, large enough to take the children's letters.

2 Bend the card into a cylinder. Stick the edges together at the back with tape or glue.

3 Cut a circle of card. Make a slit from the edge to the middle, then slide the edges together to make a cone to fit the top of the postbox.

EXTENSION IDEAS
- Let a child dress up and collect the post from the postbox, then deliver the letters to the children in the nursery.
- Use the postbox at when celebrating festivals and special occasions, too.

4 Make an information panel to show collection times. Let the children post their letters to their friends in time to catch the post.

7 Weather

 To extend musical awareness and creativity

 To talk about their own experiences of the weather

 To listen and respond to songs

 To be aware that there are different kinds of weather

Talk about the weather to let children share their experiences and understanding.

Pit - ter, pat - ter, pit, pat,

Lis - ten to the rain

Fal - ling in the gar - den, And

down the win-dow pane.

WHAT TO DO
- Talk about the weather. Ask the children to tell you about their favourite kinds of weather.
- Talk about the different sounds the rain makes.
- Ask the children to listen to the song. Repeat the song, making tapping noises. Encourage the children to join in.

 Try making other weather sounds using musical instruments.

8 Rainy days

Materials and preparation
- children's own outdoor clothes

 To talk about their own observations

 To participate in question-and-answer sessions

 To know that weather affects us and what we wear

Have a selection of other outdoor clothes with you when you discuss other types of weather.

Choose a wet rainy day to do this activity.

WHAT TO DO
- Ask the children to collect the coats they wore to the nursery.
- Ask if anybody got wet on their way to the nursery. If not, ask how they managed to stay dry.
- Consider with the children what they would wear if it was snowing/sunny/windy as they came to nursery.

Questions
- Which parts of your body got wet?
- Which parts of your body stayed dry?
- Why?

9 Keeping dry

Materials and preparation
- a selection of umbrellas • watering can
- stiff card for umbrella shapes • thread
- colouring pencils and wax crayons
- scissors • glue

 To talk about their observations

 To recognise colours and recreate patterns

 To handle objects and materials with increasing control

Questions
- Why do you need to be able to fold up umbrellas.
- How do you know when it is raining.
- What happens to drops of rain on an umbrella?

Make simple umbrella mobiles.

WHAT TO DO
- Have a collection of umbrellas to show the children. Talk about the different colours and designs. Go outside and test the umbrellas using a watering can. Watch what happens to the water on the umbrellas.
- Give each child an umbrella shape. Ask them to decorate their umbrella with a pattern, for example, stripes and spots. Talk about the colours and patterns the children use for their umbrellas. Add card handles and thread from which to hang the mobiles from the ceiling.

10 Is it waterproof?

Materials and preparation
- different fabrics/materials - some waterproof, others not (e.g. cotton, wool, PVC, towelling, etc.)

 To sort objects according to set criteria

 To explore materials and talk about their observations

EXTENSION IDEA
Ask the children to bring in some rain hats and other types of hat from home. Discuss when would be a good time to wear them.

This activity is ideal for a wet day when children can test the waterproof properties of different clothes.

WHAT TO DO
- Show the children a piece of material. Pass it around for them to see and feel. Ask them to tell you what they think would happen if water was put on it.
- Let the children drop some water onto the material. Ask them to describe what happens. Repeat with the other materials.
- Ask the children to identify the materials that soaked up the water. Ask them to tell you what happened to the water on the other materials.
- Group the materials according to whether they are waterproof or not. Ask which materials would be good/bad to use for a rain hat?

11 Keeping cool

This activity helps children to think about keeping cool and protecting themselves from the sun.

Materials and preparation
- a selection of objects that protect us from the sun or keep us cool (eg sun block, hats, sunglasses, fans, parasol)
- paper • colour pencils or wax crayons

 To talk about past experiences of the weather

 To handle materials with increasing control

 To participate in group activities led by an adult. To solve simple practical problems

 To be aware of the dangers of the sun. To explore materials and use skills such as folding

▶ WHAT TO DO
- Show the children the objects. Let them try on the hats, sunglasses, etc. Ask them when the items are used. Talk about the importance of protecting ourselves from the sun.
- Ask the children to think of other ways of keeping cool (e.g. having a drink, eating an ice cream, wearing summer clothes.
- Introduce the idea of making a fan. Show the children how to fold the paper concertina style to make a fan. Let them decorate the fans. Encourage them to test the fans by waving them close to their face.

12 Which clothes?

The purpose of this activity is to establish how the weather influences which clothes we decide to wear.

Materials and preparation
- a selection of warm and cold weather clothes in a box • dolls and some dolls' clothes • sorting rings or hoops

 To use fine motor skills to dress and undress a doll

 To be able to sort objects

 To know that weather affects us and what we wear

▶ WHAT TO DO
- Talk about the clothes the children wore on their way to nursery. Ask what they would have worn if the weather had been different.
- Ask the children to help sort the box of clothes into two piles – one of clothes for warm weather and one for cold weather.
- Let the children take it in turns to take an item of clothing out of the box.
- Ask them to say which pile they think it belongs in. Ask the rest of the group what they think.
- Talk about the clothes that might belong in both piles. Continue the activity until all the clothes have been removed from the box.

EXTENSION IDEA
Ask the children to sort some dolls' clothes into two piles, one for warm weather and one for cold weather. Let the children dress the dolls accordingly.

13 Finding out about the wind

Materials and preparation
- a selection of simple wind testers

To observe and describe changes in the weather

To explore features of the natural world.
To talk about their observations

👍 Use this activity before the kite-making activity when children can also study the wind.

Questions

How do you know if it is windy?
Can you see the wind?
How windy is it today?
Is there a strong or light breeze today, or is there no breeze at all?

An outdoor activity in which children can investigate the wind.

▶ **WHAT TO DO**

- Take a small group of children outside on a breezy day. Use simple wind testers to see how windy it is, such as a balloon on a string, a windmill, a streamer or a paper fish on the ground.
- Watch what happens to the wind testers. Ask the children to tell you what they think is happening.
- Look around to observe other effects of the wind, such as tree branches moving. Ask the children if they can feel the wind blowing against them.
- Try the wind testers again on a day when the weather is more/less windy than before. Ask the children if they notice the difference.

14 I can see a rainbow

Materials and preparation
- thin paint (red, orange, yellow, green, blue, indigo and violet) • water
- sponge • brushes • white paper

To talk about the weather

To explore properties of paint and water

To talk about their observations

Children will have fun painting rainbows while they learn about colours.

Red and yel-low and pink and green, Purple and o-range and

blue, I can sing a rainbow, Sing a rainbow,

Sing a rainbow, too.

▶ **WHAT TO DO**

- Teach the children the song 'Sing a Rainbow'.
- Talk about the shape of a rainbow and its different colours.
- Show the children how to make rainbow patterns. Use a clean sponge to dampen the sheets of paper. Make the rainbow patterns by painting stripes of different colours on the wet paper. Ask the children to watch the colours running into each other.
- Let the paint dry, then make a display with all the paintings.

Resources

The resources section provides a useful range of material to supplement the activities in this book. The booklist below contains a selection of stories, information books, songs and action rhymes. Although many of the information books are appropriate for slightly older childre, they provide a lots of useful information and high-quality illustrations. This section also contains a template to assist with making the fire-fighter's hat on page 63, you will find a template for making the fire-fighter's hat on page 30 and the index on page 64 lists all the activities in **All About My Neighbourhood**.

Story books

'Alfie Gets in First', Shirley Hughes. Red Fox.
'Don't Forget the Bacon', Pat Hutchins. Bodley Head.
'Going to Playschool', Sarah Garland. Puffin Books.
'In the Small, Small Pond', Denise Fleming. Red Fox.
'In the Tall Tall Grass', Denise Fleming. Red Fox.
'Little Red Riding Hood', Retold by Sam McBratney. McDonald Young Books.
'Miss Brick the Builder's Baby', Allan Ahlberg and Colin McNaughton. Puffin Books.
'Moving Molly', Shirley Hughes. Random Century.
'Mrs Wobble the Waitress', Allan and Janet Ahlberg. Puffin Books.
'Peepo', Janet and Allan Ahlberg. Puffin Books.
'Starting School', Janet and Allan Ahlberg. Picture Puffins.
'Six Dinner Sid', Inga Moore. Simon and Schuster Young Books.
'Tales from Percy's Park', Nick Butterworth. Harper Collins.
'The Jolly Christmas Postman', Janet and Allan Ahlberg. Heinemann.
'The Jolly Postman', Janet and Allan Ahlberg. Heinemann.
'The Snowman', Raymond Briggs. Picture Puffins.
'The Three Little Pigs', Erik Blegval. Julia MacRae Books.
'The Train Ride', June Crebbin. Walker Books.
'This is the Bear and the Scary Night', Sarah Hayes. Walker Books.
'Tom and Pippo Go for a Walk', Helen Oxenbury. Walker Books.
'Tom and Pippo Go Shopping', Helen Oxenbury. Walker Books.
'Tom and Pippo in the Garden', Helen Oxenbury. Walker Books.

Information books

'Building Site', (Busy Places Series) Franklin Watts.
'Baker', 'Bus Driver', 'Doctor', 'Fire-Fighter', 'Nurse', 'Policeman', 'Postman'(A Day in the Life of ... Series) Franklin Watts.
'Digging Machines', A. Earl and D. Sensier. Wayland.
'Fast Food Restaurant', (Busy Places Series) Franklin Watts.
'Fire-fighters – a first word and picture book', Campbell Books.
'Hospital', (Busy Places Series) Franklin Watts.
'I am Blind', Franklin Watts.
'On a Building Site', H. Pluckrose. Franklin Watts.
'On the Move', H. Pluckrose. Franklin Watts.
'Packaging', (First Technology Series) Wayland.
'Railway Station', (Busy Places Series) Franklin Watts.
'Road Builders', B. G. Hennessy. Viking Books.
'Supermarket', (Busy Places Series) Franklin Watts.

Action rhymes

'This is my little house' in 'This Little Puffin ...' compiled by E. Matterson. Puffin Books.
'Five currant buns in a baker's shop' in 'This Little Puffin ...' compiled by E. Matterson. Puffin Books.
'There was a princess long ago' in 'This Little Puffin ...' compiled by E. Matterson. Puffin Books.

Template

Use this template to help you make the firefighter's hat on page 30.

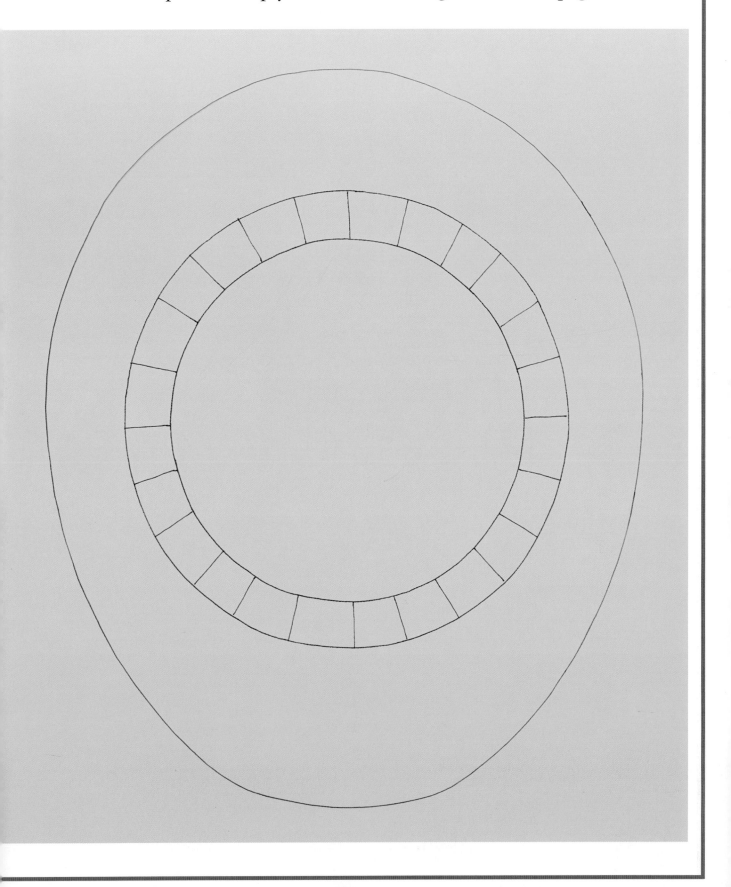

Index

A, B, C, D
A garden in miniature (9) page 19
All aboard (4) page 48
At the doctor's (9) page 31
Being a baker (4) page 42
Bird feeder (7) page 36
Blind man's buff (2) page 55
Brick patterns (5) page 23
Bridge shapes (4) page 28
Building bridges (3) page 28
Building houses (6) page 23

E, F, G
Eating out (2) page 41
Finding out about the wind (13) page 61
Finding your way (10) page 51
Flying high (8) page 36
Fun at the park (2) page 33
Gingerbread house (8) page 24

H, I, J, K
Heavy or light? (8) page 44
Helping each other (4) page 56
Here comes the bus (6) page 49
How does your garden grow? (8) page 18
I can see a rainbow (14) page 61
I went to the shops and bought (1) page 41
I'll huff and I'll puff (9) page 25

Inside homes (2) page 21
Is it waterproof? (10) page 59
Keeping cool (11) page 60
Keeping dry (9) page 59

L, M
Leaf printing (13) page 39
Little Red Riding Hood (7) page 50
Looking at leaf textures (12) page 39
Make a den (3) page 22
Make a house (4) page 22
Make a story map (11) page 52
Make fire-fighters' hats (8) page 30
My family (6) page 17
My front door (2) page 15
My home (1) page 15
My neighbourhood (1) page 27

N, O, P
Other homes (1) page 21
Our friends (3) page 56
Packaging (6) page 43
People carriers (2) page 47
Photograph puzzles (5) page 29
Piggy storyboard (10) page 25
Posting letters (6) page 57

Q, R, S
Rainy days (8) page 58
Rough or smooth? (4) page 16
Round or long? (7) page 44
Shopping bags (10) page 45
Shopping lists (9) page 45
Similar sounds (10) page 37
Simple house cards (7) page 18
Slides in the park (3) page 34
Sounds (9) page 37
Special clothes (5) page 57

T, U, V
Tall towers (2) page 27
The baker's shop (3) page 42
The park (1) page 33
The wheels on the bus (5) page 49
These people help us (7) page 30
This is my little house (5) page 17
Through my window (3) page 16
Traffic lights game (8) page 50
Traffic lights pattern (9) page 51
Traffic watching (1) page 47
Trains, boats and aeroplanes (3) page 48
Travel agents (13) page 53
Unusual homes (7) page 24
Visiting a postbox (10) page 31

W, X, Y, Z
Weather (7) page 58
What makes the best slide? (4) page 34
What's missing? (6) page 29
Where do they live? (5) page 35
Which clothes? (12) page 60
Which comes first? (1) page 55
Which shop? (5) page 43
Who lives in the park? (6) page 35
Wild animal picnic (11) page 38
Words everywhere (12) page 52

Acknowledgments

Nursery World would like to thank:

Hope Education for providing many of the props used in this book; Clare Shedden for additional design; Andy Moss for props; Colin Bunner and Alternative View Studios for digital artwork; Denise Blake for picture research; Lucy Tizard for the photograph top of page 31; Maya Kardum for the photograph top left on page 49; Sing a Rainbow, words and music by Arthur Hamilton © 1965 Warner Chappell Music Inc., USA Warner/Chappell Music Ltd, London W6 8BS Reproduced by permission of IMP Ltd.

Every effort has been made to trace the copyright holders. Times Supplements apologises for any unintentional omissions and would be pleased, in such cases, to add an acknowledgment in future editions.